FIRE
NITRO
RUBBER
AND
SMOKE

Bob McClurg's
Drag Racing Memories

CarTech®

Edited by Peter Bodensteiner

Designed by Katie Sonmor

ISBN-13 978-1-932494-37-2
ISBN-10 1-932494-37-5

Printed in China

CarTech®

39966 Grand Avenue
North Branch, MN 55056
Telephone: (651) 277-1200 or (800) 551-4754
Fax: (651) 277-1203
www.cartechbooks.com

Library of Congress Cataloging-in-Publication Data

McClurg, Bob.
 Fire, nitro, rubber, and smoke : Bob McClurg's drag racing memories / by Bob McClurg.
 p. cm.
 ISBN-13: 978-1-932494-37-2
 ISBN-10: 1-932494-37-5
 1. Drag racing--United States--History. 2. Automobiles, Racing--United States--History. 3. Drag racers--United States. I. Title. II. Title: Bob McClurg's drag racing memories.

 GV1029.3.M38 2006
 796.72--dc22
                                        2006025615

Cover:
This car is from the Brooklyn, Michigan-based Fighting Irish Top Fuel team of Beebe & Murphy, an extension of the original Southern California-based Beebe Bros., Vinson & Sixt Top Fuel team from the early 1960s. Tim "Chops" Beebe and Jim "Holy Smokes" Murphy joined forces in the early 1970s to campaign the Beebe & Murphy Fighting Irish rear-engine AA/FDs (there were two), which primarily competed on the UDRA Midwest circuit. In fact, Beebe & Murphy were the 1973 circuit champs.

Cover inset:
Rich Guasco's small-block Chevrolet-powered *Pure Hell* AA/FA, with Dale "Snail" Emery behind the wheel, won the AA/HR class at the 1964 *Hot Rod* Magazine Championship Drag Races at Riverside International Raceway. Photo by G.K. Callaway

Front flap:
Here's a classic match-up between Ron Nunes' Chrysler-powered (yeah, it still says "Oldsmobile" on the hood) '41 Willys AA/GS against Bob "Bones" Balogh in the Bones, Dubach & Pisano AA/GS '33 Willys coupe at the *Hot Rod* Magazine Championship Drag Races at Riverside International Raceway in June 1966. Judging from the photo, it's pretty easy to guess who won. Photo by G.K. Callaway

Title page:
Author Bob McClurg's favorite "Dyno Don" Nicholson car was his candy apple red '66 Logghe-chassis *Eliminator II*, which won its first eight races straight. The addition of a supercharger helped the car run in the 7.90s at 181+ mph by season's end.

Back cover:
Jack Mitchell and the Rockford, Illinois, team of Mitchell, Hay & Klentz, were among the last to campaign a front-engine Top Fuel car. This overhead shot clearly demonstrates that they had made the switch to a rear-engine car by 1975.

OVERSEAS DISTRIBUTION BY:

Brooklands Books Ltd.
P.O. Box 146, Cobham, Surrey, KT11 1LG, England
Telephone 01932 865051 • Fax 01932 868803
www.brooklands-books.com

Brooklands Books Australia
3/37-39 Green Street, Banksmeadow, NSW 2019, Australia
Telephone 2 9695 7055 • Fax 2 9695 7355

CONTENTS

DEDICATION

This book is dedicated to the lasting memories of Kevin Boales, Malcolm Durham, Cloyce C.J. "Pappy" Hart, Cecil "Brand-X Racing" Lankford, Victor McClurg, Sush Matsubara, "Big John" Mazmanian, Gene Mooneyham, Tony "Loner" Nancy, "Dyno Don" Nicholson, Barbara L. Parks, Ronnie Roseberry, Mark Richter, and Ronnie Sox.

ACKNOWLEDGMENTS

I thank Greg Sharp, curator of the Wally Parks NHRA Motorsports Museum, for his historical input and sage advice. Furthermore, no one—including myself—knows everything about what happened back in "the good old days," so I also thank Chris Martin for writing *The Top Fuel Handbook*; the National Hot Rod Association (NHRA) for their extremely handy media guides; and Michael Mikulice, who co-authored *Big Daddy: A Career Pictorial*, volumes one through three. These books are available through your local automotive book retailer.

I also want to acknowledge the efforts of co-contributor George "G.K." Callaway, a close friend of mine and one of early drag racing's most talented and unsung photojournalists. An aerospace engineer by trade, Callaway was also a key figure at Deist Safety Equipment in the mid 1960s and worked closely with Jim Deist on a number of safety innovations. While I was sitting up in the grandstand, still wet behind the ears, G.K. was out there on the starting line capturing 1960s drag racing at its finest. G.K. also distinguished himself as a driver of note on the 1964–'65 Mobil Gas Economy Runs and worked with Bill Fredricks on rocket car projects like the *Courage of Australia* and the *Armor All Rocket*. G.K. is also a multi-land speed record holder in the roadster class, driving a Toyota-powered 1929 Model A highboy, and is currently working on a Honda-powered land speed record car.

Of course, G.K.'s work was extensively showcased in *Diggers, Funnies, Gassers & Altereds*. And, once again, G.K. (a.k.a. the Mayor of El Mirage) and I have managed to come up with a whole bunch more previously unpublished G.K. Callaway drag racing action photos to contribute to this effort, which the two of us humorously like to refer to as *The Burnout Book!*

Of course, when you're dealing with delicate 40-year-old drag racing photographs and transparencies, sometimes a little Adobe Photoshop is necessary to return these images to their former splendor. I thank graphic artist Donny Sarian (www.sarian.com) for all his invaluable assistance in this regard.

—Bob McClurg

ABOUT THE AUTHOR

Bob McClurg grew up in 1950s Southern California, where as a lad he was constantly influenced by hot rods and the hot rod culture. It was all around him!

In his pre-teen days, McClurg shined shoes at Towne Barber Shop on Chapman Avenue in the city of Orange, where there were always plenty of copies of *Hot Rod* magazine laying around to read. Or, if he wanted to look at the real thing, all he had to do was walk a half a block north and hang out at a place called Hart Automotive, owned by famed drag racing pioneer Jack Hart, who went on to become the first competition director for the fledgling NHRA. Two blocks north of Batavia Street on Chapman was a hamburger hangout known as Jerry & Ivan's Drive-In, one of the hottest cruising spots in Orange County during the 1950s. If that didn't send a kid of 11 into sensory overload, two blocks up Chapman Avenue across the railroad tracks were both the Bill Corwin Ford and the Selman Chevrolet new car dealerships, and the local Goodyear tire re-treading shop. Yeah, growing up in sunny "So Cal" was a lot of fun in those days!

"In my parochial school days, I had written a piece on traffic safety that had attracted the attention of the editor of the *Orange Daily News*," McClurg said. "Once I got to junior high, that aging piece of newsprint was good enough to land me a job as the editor of the McPherson Jr. High School newspaper. Unfortunately, it quickly became apparent to everyone involved that one single, solitary newspaper article did not qualify me as a Pulitzer Prize-winning journalist. The editor's job lasted for about six weeks before I was deposed!"

In the early 1960s, McClurg's family relocated across town to rural Villa Park, where he pursued his goal to become a writer while attending school at the Orange Unified School District's newly opened Villa Park High School. About the same time, McClurg's uncle Victor McClurg sent him his old Argus C3 35-mm camera. However, because McClurg wasn't all that good at mathematics, he didn't embrace the mechanics of photography quickly.

In the fall of 1964, McClurg enrolled in Villa Park High School's yearbook class thinking he would land a job as a staff writer. Unfortunately, by that time all the writer's jobs had already been filled.

"My instructor's name was John Osborn," McClurg recalled. "He was one of those old school journalism teachers in the true 'stop-the-presses' tradition. His advice was simple: Either take the photographer's job, or transfer!" McClurg reluctantly started taking pictures.

"At first, it was purely a hit and miss proposition. Then a gentleman named Dick Gould of the Orange Photo Studio took me under his wing. Dick had the senior-picture contract with the school, and part of the deal was that he would train the yearbook photographic staff and provide them with black and white film.

"I can honestly say that I greatly enjoyed the experience. A yearbook photo shoot was always good for legally cutting a class or two while photographing everything from varsity football to the latest gadget they were building in wood shop." However, McClurg never entertained the notion that perhaps he could actually become a full-time photojournalist.

Then one foggy night in 1964 Bob snuck out on the starting line at Lions Associated Drag Strip with the school's Yashica LM 120 camera. By his own admission, the images he recorded on film that cold, foggy Long Beach evening were meager at best. However, they provided the inspiration for McClurg to pursue an active career in automotive photojournalism, and quite frankly, we here at CarTech are glad that he did.

This book is Bob McClurg's third CarTech title. However, it might also be considered a sequel to Bob's best-selling first effort, *Diggers, Funnies, Gassers & Altereds*, which was awarded an International Automotive Media Award in November 2004.

Bob also set aside enough time to write the tech book, *How to Build Supercharged and Turbocharged Small-Block Fords*, which is quite fitting because high-performance Fords just so happen to be McClurg's other all-consuming passion.

INTRODUCTION

This is more than just a coffee-table picture book—it's a book chock full of my drag racing memories.

From my earliest days reading copies of *Hot Rod* magazine while shining shoes at the Towne Barber Shop, to my later years hanging out at shops like Anaheim Speed Engineering, Bill Thomas Race Cars, Doug's Headers, and Von Fritch Automotive, my interest in fast cars and hot rods in particular was almost insatiable. For as long as I can remember, I always wanted to become involved with drag racing, although I must admit that as an adolescent, I never envisioned that it would be from a journalistic standpoint.

My love of cars was also fueled by the fact that I was born chronically asthmatic and could not participate in traditional stick-and-ball sports like most young boys my age. So, I could either become an egghead or a gear head. Fortunately, I chose the latter.

When I was just 13 years old, I worked for a gentleman named Roger Clausen, the owner of Gish's Toys & Hobbies, located in the City of Orange. Slot car racing was the hottest thing going in those days, and Clausen owned one of the nicest slot car tracks in town. Since I was on half-day sessions at Orange High School, where I was a lowly sophomore, I often worked for Clausen in the morning before going to school. One Saturday, he asked me if I would like to accompany him that evening to a Top Fuel race at Lions. It seemed that old Clausen was a "Big Daddy" Don Garlits fan. In fact, he was an absolute Garlits fanatic!

"Garlits will be there with his winged fueler (*Swamp Rat V-B*), and he'll be racing guys like the "Greek" Chris Karamesines," Don "Snake" Prudhomme, and others," Roger said. "You gotta come!"

I can honestly say that my first experience at the drags was nothing short of incredible. The sights, the sounds, and the smells that typified Southern California drag racing back in the early 1960s were absolutely mind-boggling! Lions Associated Drag Strip was the best place in the world to experience all those sensations in one sitting—sensations, I might add, you could never experience by reading any hot rod magazine.

Likewise, I'll never forget attending my first national event, the NHRA Winternationals in February 1964, but for an entirely different reason. Those were the days when you were permitted to sleep overnight in your car along Arrow Highway, White Avenue, or McKinley Avenue, and this was a happening in itself. I remember my brother-in-law Wes Hays and a friend of his had just installed a brand new Hurst shifter in his '60 Chevy Biscayne. With two grown-ups and

In 1964, it didn't matter whether it was Top Fuel or Top Gas, this was the car to beat in national event competition. "Big Daddy" Don Garlits' notorious *Wynn's Jammer*, or *Swamp Rat VI-A*, won Top Gas at Indy in 1964. It was also runner-up to Conrad "Connie" Kalitta at the U.S. Fuel and Gas Championships at Bakersfield in 1964 running on fuel. Moreover, this car was the ultimate match race champion, winning races all over the United States, producing a career best of 8.02-194.30.

In late 1964, Garlits' *Wynn's Jammer* also toured England as part of the United States Drag Racing Team. Garlits made drag racing history the following year when he totally dominated the 1965 U.S. Fuel & Gas Championships with a three-car Top Fuel assault. The effort was spearheaded by Garlits, along with co-drivers Connie Swingle and "Starvin Marvin" Schwartz. Ultimately, Garlits defeated Ed Pink's *Old Master* in the final with Mike "Hawaiian" Snively at the wheel. Today, *Swamp Rat V1-A* has been restored, and when it isn't on display at the Don Garlits Museum of Drag Racing, it's on loan to museums like the Wally Parks NHRA Motorsports Museum or the Petersen Automotive Museum. Photo by G.K. Callaway

one "kid" cramped inside a two-door Chevy, I found myself sleeping across the transmission hump! Going to the Winternationals, though, was a good enough trade for a night of discomfort. Once there, I saw first-hand many of the big names I had only read about: "Big John" Mazmanian, Stone, Woods & Cook, Sox & Martin, Tony "Loner" Nancy, "Dyno Don" Nicholson, Hugh Tucker—they were all there!

During my senior year in high school (1965–'66), I was off to the drag races on a daily basis. A friend named Dave Harrell used to own a '30 Model A Ford Tudor Sedan, which he found parked out in the orange groves of Villa Park. Since Dave already had his California driver's license, he and I would jump in his A-bone and drive out to Lions practically every Saturday. In exchange for the ride, I would pay for the gas, all the eats, and the pit passes. Heck of a deal, huh?

In late 1966, my old friend, Chevrolet star Hayden "Old Folks" Proffitt, was given the opportunity to rescue the faltering Grant Rambler Rebel SST Funny Car program, which had been started by "Banzai Bill" Haines. Early tests indicated that a poorly designed chassis was the main reason the car wouldn't go straight. So Hayden took the chassis from his half-completed '67 Camaro Funny Car and married it to the Grant Rambler Rebel SST bodywork. Suddenly, the car started performing like it should. This photo was taken at Indianapolis 1967, where the Grant Rambler Rebel SST ran 8.50s at 172.00 and dispatched none other than "Dyno Don" Nicholson and his *Eliminator 1* Mercury Comet. Later, a huge wheel stand ruined Proffitt's day. Photo by G.K. Callaway

With a stock '30 Model-A four banger wheezing away underneath the hood (barring any unforeseen mechanical problems that always seemed to occur at the most inopportune times), it took quite awhile to get to Lions. Those were the days before the Garden Grove Freeway was built. I remember taking Katella Avenue west to Los Alamitos where we would pick up the San Diego Freeway north. We would jump into the slow lane and drive at the breakneck speed of 45 mph until we reached Wilmington's Alameda Avenue off-ramp. Of course, we never realized we were taking our lives into our own hands with each ensuing journey. After all, we were young and bulletproof. All we wanted to do was go to the drag races!

During one of those weekend excursions out to Lions I brought along the high school yearbook's Yashica LM 120 camera, and I shot a roll of black and white film from the bleachers. Looking back, the stuff was pretty bad. However, what I recorded on film that night provided the impetus to actively pursue this newfound passion. During ensuing trips to Long Beach I often snuck out onto the starting line to grab what shots I could, only to be escorted off by Lions publicist, and one of the sport's finest drag racing photojournalists, "Digger Ralph" Guldahl.

"Kid, I can't let you out here without a letter of assignment from the editor of either a newspaper or a magazine," Guldahl always said.

Finally, in the summer of 1966, I hooked up with the sports editor at the *Orange Daily News* and convinced him to write me a letter of assignment. Because the guy was being drafted into the Army and was leaving for boot camp the following week, he was more than happy to oblige. That first letter gained me my much-desired Lions starting line photo access pass just in time to attend the 1966 Professional Dragster Association (PDA) Championships. Don "Snake" Prudhomme won the event handily, driving the Brand Motors Ford Special AA/FD.

About that time, I also developed a friendship with one of my all-time heroes, Chevrolet match race star Hayden Proffitt. After getting a piece published in *Super Stock & Drag Illustrated* magazine's "Match Race Madness" column when Hayden and his S/XS Corvair defeated "Fast Eddie" Schartman's Comet three straight at Lions (I remember carrying a copy of that magazine around in my back pocket for months), Proffitt put in a good word for me with the editors at *Drag Strip* magazine, and I was given credentials to attend the DRM East Versus West Funny Car Championships, again held at Lions. It was an event that Hayden won easily.

Of course, there was an ongoing dues-paying process I went through with the other photographers at the local tracks, who generally regarded me as an interloper. I also had to fight to gain legitimacy with the strip promoters up and down the West Coast (i.e., Northern California's Fremont and Sears Point Raceways, and Southern California's Irwindale and Carlsbad Raceways), who guarded the photo passes as if they were the keys to Fort Knox. But once my work started to appear in local newspapers like the *Anaheim Bulletin* and the *Los Angeles Times* Orange County Bureau, things began to loosen up.

In the interim, I also shot quite a lot of high school and college football as well as tons of nasty, mainstream stuff (such as murders, plane crashes, shopping center grand openings, and bar mitzvahs) to collect a paycheck and to appease the newspaper editors. Throughout it all, I never veered from my intended goal: to become a professional drag racing photographer. Then on August 10, 1967, Orange County International Raceway (OCIR) opened its doors, and my life really changed.

OCIR was one of the nation's first "super tracks," and it was located just a stone's throw away from where I lived. Having my own drag strip proved a real plus to honing my craft, and I was even able to pinch-hit for OCIR strip

photographer "Diamond Jim" Kelly on several occasions. And that, too, proved to be a learning experience.

One Tuesday morning after covering a race I received a terse telephone call from OCIR publicist and track announcer Paul Culley, who was less than impressed with my coverage in that week's issue of *Drag News*.

"Bob, nobody wants to see single photos of race cars going down the track. They want to see race coverage. That means two cars in the picture, side-by-side, racing each other. Get it?"

It was a point well taken. Up until that time, I had been concentrating on just getting the cars properly framed, in focus, and stopping the action. I had totally overlooked the big picture.

In the fall of 1967, I redeemed myself with my first cover. The photo was of "Fast Eddie" Schartman in action (with the OCIR tower in the background) and Schartman's incredible *Air Lift Rattler* 1967 Mercury Comet winning OCIR's inaugural Manufacturer's Funny Car Team Championships.

About the same time, gravy jobs like photographing the winner's circle pictures for NHRA at both the 1967 and 1968 NHRA Winternationals started coming in, and some of the big companies like Fram (upon recommendation from my dear departed friend Leslie Lovett) started noticing my work. Shooting the 1968 U.S. Nationals at Indy for Fram was probably one of the greatest experiences of all. Through Fram's

Frank McGonagle and his staff, I was able to meet and greet many of my heroes like "Big Daddy" Don Garlits, Linda Vaughn (aka "Miss Hurst Golden Shifter"), Sox & Martin, "Dandy" Dick Landy, and numerous others.

My Indy exploits eventually led to a full-time job as photo editor at *Super Stock & Drag Illustrated* magazine in April 1969. Those were some really great times, working with the likes of Jim Davis, Jim McCraw, and Ro McGonegal, all of whom I remain in contact with to this day. Furthermore, being that SS&DI's parent organization, Eastern Publishing Company, was based in Alexandria, Virginia, I finally got to see what eastern drag racing was all about.

Unfortunately, a mid-year change in ownership at SS&DI radically deteriorated the working environment. Realizing that if I really wanted to learn how to write properly, I needed to return to college. I eventually obtained an A.A. degree in photojournalism. The Hasselblad photographic equipment I owned turned out to be nicer than the cameras owned by some of my photo instructors, which caused some jealousy issues.

During one of his rare IHRA appearances, "Dandy Dick" Landy charged off the IHRA Rockingham Dragway starting line. Landy's Dodge Demon ran as quick as a 9.12 in legal trim and even quicker with the weight out.

Aside from both being seeded AHRA cars, "Big Daddy" Don Garlits and Jim "Superman" Nicoll also shared the frustration of having had their cars cut in half by clutch and transmission explosions. Nicoll's separation came at the 1970 NHRA U.S. Nationals where he raced Don "Snake" Prudhomme in the final—6.45-230.76 versus a 6.48-225.56. When the clutch let go and Nicoll's car was cut in half, the back half of his car was sent bouncing along the guardrail through the lights. Thinking that he had won the race, he climbed out of the severed digger hollering, "I won, I won," only to discover that he had lit the big red bulb back at the starting line. Talk about complete and total humiliation!

In the winter of 1969, I began expanding my sphere of influence traveling outside California to places like the 1969 AHRA World Finals held at Beeline Dragway in Arizona. Based off the work produced from this and other events, I began a successful run with *Hot Rod* magazine, selling numerous Racing Gallery center spreads and single pagers, all the while saving up enough money to buy my first new car, a '71 Mercury Capri.

The summer of 1970 marked the first of many road tours with the Capri, which included attending the NHRA U.S. Nationals at Indy. There I witnessed the first ever Top Fuel blow-over in NHRA national event history by Jimmy King (King & Marshall), as well as the topsy-turvy Top Fuel finale between Jim "Superman" Nicoll and Don "Snake" Prudhomme.

Money was very tight in those days, and I seized every opportunity I could to grab a free ride to a national event, in spite of the fact that on numerous occasions I didn't have even the slightest inkling of how I was going to get back home again. For example, longtime friend "Dandy Dick" Landy allowed me to hitch rides in his Chrysler Performance Clinic truck to both the 1971 NHRA Gatornationals and NHRA Springnationals events. However, Landy had post-race

clinic engagements elsewhere on the eastern seaboard, which prohibited me from hitching a ride back home again. I ended up taking a Greyhound bus back home instead.

In the early 1970s, I often co-drove a Ryder truck packed full of NHRA's timing equipment to national events like Indy, Columbus, Dallas, Amarillo, and Englishtown. This was a couple of years before the NHRA had re-established its "Safety Safari" national event support team, and I was often accompanied by the likes of NHRA Technical Director Bill "Farmer" Dismuke, as well as *National DRAGSTER* staffers John Joduga and Bill Crites. My willingness to lend a helping hand often put me in good stead with the folks at National Wally, as the NHRA was often called in those days. Once at the race I would stay at the host hotel as an NHRA guest, which not only saved me a ton of money but also got me the right photo passes. More often than not I would also assist NHRA photo director Leslie Lovett out on the starting line and pick up a couple of extra bucks in the process.

In 1972, I also briefly held the position as public relations director for up-and-coming Chrysler Pro Stock contender Bobby Yowell (N.T. Yowell Movers Racing Team; Dayton, Ohio), which proved a real eye-opener the minute I

Bobby Yowell of Dayton, Ohio, raced a number of Sox & Martin-built Plymouth Duster customer cars from 1970 to 1973, twice winning the NHRA Division 3 Pro Stock points championship. Perhaps Yowell's finest hour came at the 1972 IHRA Pro Am at Rockingham, North Carolina, where he was runner-up to Mike Fons in the Rod Shop Dodge in the final, recording a best of 9.67-143.00 on the back bumper. In the spring of 1972, I became Yowell's P.R. man and traveled with the team throughout the season. Aside from on-track performances like Rockingham, we also won "Best Appearing Crew" honors at that event as well as at the NHRA Summernationals at Raceway Park, shown here in this black and white photo. I'm on the far right. Unfortunately, the politics of Pro Stock Eliminator, especially when dealing with the folks at Chrysler, really weren't my cup of tea, so I left the team in November 1972 and returned to freelancing. Black & white photo courtesy Steve Reyes

became involved. The inner workings of Chrysler-sponsored NHRA/IHRA Pro Stock racing were politically charged.

The following year I returned to freelancing, spending much of my time traveling to NHRA and IHRA national events. In 1973, I became the official photographer/writer/publicist for the IHRA, covering its national event series. That meant that I would work all day out at the racetrack and then rush back to the motel that night, develop the film, and make the prints. Sunday evening I would work all night typing the event coverage, developing the film, and making all the prints. Then I would rush the results to tabloids like *Motorsports Weekly*, *Drag Times*, and *Drag News*. That was some of the hardest work I have ever done.

When I wasn't traveling the IHRA circuit I began shooting car features for publications like Petersen Publishing's book division and *Cars* magazine, who by the mid-1970s had appointed me its West Coast editor. Those early days as a freelancer are fondly remembered, and I often re-live them with some of my old cronies at events like the

Wally Parks NHRA Motorsports Museum-hosted California Hot Rod Reunion.

I used to frequently travel to events with legendary crash-and-burn photojournalist Steve Reyes (author of *Quarter-Mile Chaos* and the upcoming *Funny Car Fever*), who along with "Diamond Jim" Kelly, Jon Asher, Mert Miller, Alan Earman, Tom West, Barry Wiggens, and others were making names for themselves as "shooters." We often called East Coast photographer Jeff Tinsley's Silver Springs, Maryland, home (Tinsley was a photo editor at SS&DI and later joined the Smithsonian Institution's photographic staff), which was our base of operations while photographing summer events throughout the eastern seaboard. To save money, we often shared motel rooms, piling as many as six of us into one single room.

In 1976, I accepted a job as photo editor with Petersen's specialty publications division, working with Lee Kelley, "200 MPH" Dave Wallace Jr., Ron Cogan, Davis Hetzler, and Eric Pierce, launching such titles as *Hot Rod Drag Racing*, *Kit*

Car, Four Wheel & Off Road, and Pickups & Mini Trucks. The following year I graduated to photo editor at Hot Rod Magazine, and held that position until 1979. In the process I was fortunate enough to have worked with two of my all-time publishing industry heroes: former Hot Rod magazine Photo Editor Eric "Rick" Rickman, whose work I had admired all the way back to my shoeshine days, and Gray "Yer Old Dad" Baskerville, one of the finest automotive writers ever known.

After my time at Hot Rod, I tried some more public relations work as well as photography work for the motion picture and recording industries. By 1982, though, I regained my senses and escaped from the rock and roll business, returning to Petersen Publishing Company to accept the job as editor, first for Petersen's Corvette Annual and later for Petersen's Kit Car.

In 1986, I accepted the job as editor for McMullen & Yee Publishing Company's (aka McMullen/Argus) Mustang Illustrated magazine. Seven years later, Ford High Performance magazine was launched, and I edited each on alternating months until my departure from the company in 1998. During my tenure at McMullen & Yee, I worked on two of the most exciting projects of my entire automotive career. The first was as a freelance consultant on the design and development of the 1994-2004 Ford Mustang, code name "SN-95." In the process I wrote the book, Mustang: The Next Generation, documenting the car's creation, start to finish. The book was officially licensed by Ford and eventually became a best-seller. The second project was my involvement with Team Saleen at the 1998 24 Hours of Le Mans, where I spent 10 days in the French countryside with Mustang maven Steve Saleen and his two-car Mustang team.

Also while at McMullen & Yee, I was asked by former Popular Hot Rodding magazine editor Randy Fish to display some of my best vintage drag racing work in a special monthly section of Popular Hot Rodding called "Back Trackin'." Ultimately, this page turned out to be one of Popular Hot Rodding's most popular departments, and its success prompted the writing of my first CarTech title, Diggers, Funnies, Gassers & Altereds: Drag Racing's Golden Era.

I've been asked on numerous occasions why I don't still actively photograph drag racing. The reasons are many. When I was photographing the sport in the early days, things weren't nearly as structured and as politically charged as they are today. Photographers had more freedom than they do today, which tended to encourage photographic experimentation and creativity. Granted, some of the stuff we did back in the old days was a little crazy, like climbing up on top of the guardrail, shooting off the top of a 10-foot stepladder, shooting heat wave shots underneath the guardrails (which have since been replaced by concrete barriers), and even standing out on the racetrack shooting "head-ons." Sure, you had to run for your life every once in awhile, but as a 23-year-old kid armed with a Hasselblad 120 camera, a 250-mm telephoto lens, and a starting line photo credential, I didn't mind. With today's stringent insurance regulations, major sanctioning bodies won't tolerate these activities. I still get my fix, though, at least twice a year at the Wally Parks NHRA Motorsports Museum's California Hot Rod Reunion and NHRA Hot Rod Reunion held in Bowling Green, Kentucky, where I can re-live the good old days, sell a few books and posters, and see old friends again.

The year 2006 marked my 40th anniversary as an automotive journalist, and I have many drag racing memories to share in this book. For example, I remember my late wife Barbara telling me how she would baby-sit Keith Black's two children while Keith, Tom Greer, and Don "Snake" Prudhomme warmed up the Greer, Black & Prudhomme AA/FD out on Lynwood, California's Tenaya Street. I also remember when Bruce Wheeler, Bud Reese, and I almost went to jail for photographing a feature on the Wheeler Dealer II Top Fuel car on, unbeknownst to us, federal property in Washington, D.C. There was also the time when Leonard Hughes and I drove his ramp truck down a D.C. Parkway and almost got the Candies & Hughes Barracuda Funny Car confiscated by the D.C. Parkway cops.

Then there are the memories of the touch football games the NHRA event staff used to have at Indy before the race started, the incredible euphoria inside the winner's circle after OCIR's $14,000 Winner Take All Drag Race. There were countless weekends when we shot a Saturday night Top Fuel race at either Lions Associated Drag Strip (LADS) or Irwindale, and went home to develop the film and make prints all night. Then we'd show up at the OCIR the next morning for a Funny Car race to try and sell them.

Of course, I can't forget the time I took out 65 feet of barbed wire fence on OCIR's entry road with my Corvair while showing off for my girlfriend late one night after the drag races. Ah, the humiliation! I also remember the time "Broadway Freddie" de Name fired up his AA/Fuel Funny Car on the world famous Coney Island Boardwalk. And the time Mike Civelli and I towed "Slammin' Sammy" Miller's new Mustang rocket car from Los Angeles to Gainesville, Florida, only to have both car and trailer pass us at 70 mph in the fast lane, at three o'clock in the morning, inside the Gulfport, Mississippi, ship channel tunnel! Finally, I remember Lions' first PDA race and its last drag race almost as if both were yesterday.

All these are some of my most treasured drag racing memories and are good enough reason to produce a sequel to my first book. So instead of a historical overview with vintage action photos, Fire, Nitro, Rubber, and Smoke is a view from the trenches as seen through my eyes and of those of us who were out there on the starting line.

Chapter 1

DIGGERS

August 10, 1967, marked the opening of the sport's first Super Track, OCIR. Shown here is one of Top Fuel's winningest and best-liked teams: (James) Warren, (Roger) Coburn, and (Marvin) Miller, otherwise known as the "Ridge Route Terrors." WC&M were one of the first teams to try a slipper clutch in a Top Fuel car. In fact, WC&M and Tom "Mongoose" McEwen were the ones who showed "Big Daddy" Don Garlits how to set up his clutch at the 1967 U.S. Nationals, and Garlits showed his appreciation by dispatching McEwen in the semis and Warren in the finals. However, in local action Warren, Coburn & Miller were practically invincible. Here are just a few of their front engine Top Fuel accomplishments:

Top Speed 227.58 at inaugural PDA Championships, Lions, on July 20, 1967.

Top Speed record 230.17 on April 16, 1967, at Fresno, California.

Top Speed 229.58 on October 77, 1967, at Irwindale, California, and 230.96 at the *Hot Rod* Magazine Championship Drags in June 1968.

Top Speed 221.67 at the AHRA Winternationals at Beeline Dragway in January 1969.

Top Speed 238.15 on December 14, 1969, at Irwindale, California.

Winner of the Sunday Top Fuel segment, 1966 U.S. Fuel & Gas Championships in Bakersfield, California.

Winner Top Fuel at the 1968 NHRA Winternationals, and Top Speed of the Meet at 230.76.

Top Speed 223.32 and runner-up at the Lions Associated Drag Strip AHRA Grand American Meet in June 1969, plus a ton of local event wins. Photo by G.K. Callaway

With the suspension of NHRA's infamous fuel ban in January 1963, "T.V. Tommy" Ivo and his Kent Fuller-chassis *Barnstormer* ran as quick as 7.84-seconds at San Gabriel Raceway (February 24, 1963) as well as set the MPH record of 202.70 at Half Moon Bay on May 26, 1963. Out of all the Top Fuel cars Ivo campaigned (and there were many), the *Barnstormer* was his most memorable. In fact, Ivo took the digger to Great Britain as part of the United States Drag Racing Team in 1964, along with "Big Daddy" Don Garlits, Tony "Loner" Nancy, Dos Palmas Machine, K.S. Pittman, "Ohio George" Montgomery, Sox & Martin, and Dave Strickler. Today, at 70 years young, Ivo is retired as a driver but is still very much involved with the sport. He is an active patron of the Wally Parks NHRA Motorsports Museum in Pomona, California. He is also an inductee of the Don Garlits Museum of Drag Racing, the International Motorsports Hall of Fame, and most recently, the Motorsports Hall of Fame of America. During one of his die cast model car signing sessions at the Chet "Cyclone Headers" Knox-owned Autobooks-Aerobooks bookstore located in Burbank, California, we recently asked Ivo if he misses driving a dragster. He laughingly replied, "Heck no. Are you kidding? Have you seen the way I drive? I'm always backing into trash cans or driving over the curb. They wouldn't let me back behind the wheel of one of those things again!" Photo by "Diamond Jim" Kelly, courtesy of "T.V. Tommy" Ivo

Always the showman, former actor Tommy Ivo is seen here in the pits at Pomona Raceway explaining the finer points of a Dave Zeuschel-built 392 Chrysler Hemi Top Fuel racing engine to fellow Mouseketeer Annette Funicello. Yes, Tommy was in the original Mickey Mouse Club. The year was 1964, and Funicello, who was on loan from Walt Disney Studios and had just completed filming *Bikini Beach* for American International Pictures, posed in the pits for well-known automotive photographer Lester Nehamkin.

When I first started going to the drag races at Lions Associated Drag Strip, the Chrysler-powered, Kent Fuller-chassis, Greer, Black & Prudhomme AA/FD was the car to beat out on the West Coast. From June 1962 to November 1964, the Greer, Black & Prudhomme Top Fuel dragster with driver Don "Snake" Prudhomme at the wheel boasted an unheard of 236-7 win–loss record. In 1962 and 1963, Greer, Black & Prudhomme flat dominated Southern California's weekend Top Fuel shows. The team's numerous accomplishments included winning the first UDRA Meet at Lions on February 2, 1964, as well as taking the runner-up spot in the AA/FD class at the inaugural *Hot Rod* Magazine Drags in June 1964. Furthermore, Greer, Black & Prudhomme continuously set and re-set the low elapsed time mark during their three-year reign, clocking a career best of 7.75-seconds at San Gabriel Raceway on June 29, 1963.

Prudhomme, of course, went on to drive for Roland "The Hawaiian" Leong and Lou Baney/Ed Pink (Brand Motors Ford Special) prior to venturing out on his own in 1968. Today, he is the successful owner of the multi-car "Snake Racing" Skoal Bandit-Miller Lite Top Fuel and Funny Car team.

Of course, stories about the lightning-quick Prudhomme have practically become American folklore, but here's one we'll bet few have ever heard, much less read about. In 1949, my late wife, Barbara Kassak McClurg, and her parents moved to the West Coast from Michigan and purchased a three-bedroom home located at 3337 Tenaya Street in Lynwood, California. This just happened to be the same house where Keith Black was born. Black's father sold it to the Kassaks after he and Keith Black built a new home next door for him and his growing family. Behind the new home, father and son built a two-and-a-half-car garage, which was where the original Keith Black Racing Engines was headquartered.

As a teenager, Barbara used to baby-sit Keith Black's son Donnie (who now runs KBRE) and daughter Judy while Black and his employees worked on the GB&P Top Fuel dragster. Barbara vividly recalled that on more than one occasion the team would warm up the Greer, Black & Prudhomme Top Fuel dragster out on Tenaya Street prior to going to the drag races, right in the middle of Lynwood.

The first time Barbara told me that story I, naturally, inquired, "Did the cops ever show up?" "Never," she said. "In those days, most of the residents on Tenaya Street were employed by Keith Black Racing Engines, so nobody dared complain!" Photo by "Diamond Jim" Kelly

One of the most unique Top Fuel teams in early drag racing history was the "Surfers" entry (near camera) of Bob Skinner, Tom Jobe, and Mike Sorokin, shown here at old San Fernando opposite an unidentified Top Fuel competitor These three Santa Monica, California, racers were the last of the "Giant Killers" in front-engine Top Fuel. Considered budget racers in all respects, the Surfers' finest hour came in March 1966 at the U.S. Fuel & Gas Championships in Bakersfield, California, when they triumphed over a 64-car Top Fuel field that included the likes of James Warren, Dunn & Yates, Mike "Hawaiian" Snively, and "Terrible Ted" Gotelli. In fact, Skinner, Jobe & Sorokin defeated practically every big name front engine Top Fuel car there for three days running, starting with a 7.34-second qualifying shot on Friday and winning all the marbles on Sunday defeating Warren & Coburn in the final with a 7.74-196.06. Unfortunately, by Indy 1966, with the rising costs of competing in Top Fuel, the team was out of money, and it disbanded. In November 1967, Sorokin lost his life during a night race at OCIR when a clutch explosion cut Tony Waters' Top Fuel car in half, ultimately throwing Sorokin out of the car at 218 mph. However, the legacy Sorokin left behind is carried on today by his son Adam, who recently gained his NHRA Nostalgia Top Fuel Driver's License. Like his father did, Adam is making a name for himself as a driver among drivers. Photo by G.K. Callaway

In 1964–65, Top Fuel Eliminator became revitalized with the introduction of a number of exciting new late-model big-block V-8 engines that were originally developed for use in the factory Super Stock programs. Chevrolet had their new 396/427 Semi Hemi, or Rat Motor. Chrysler had their second generation 426 Hemi, and Ford introduced their new 427 Single Overhead Cam (SOHC) engine. The minute fuel racers like Conrad "Connie" Kalitta, "Big Daddy" Don Garlits, and the Ramchargers got their hands on these exciting new power plants, things changed quickly. Shown is Kalitta posing in the fall of 1964 with his 427 SOHC Ford-powered *Bounty Hunter* AA/FD (the first of its kind), parked in front of Ford Motor Company's "Big Glass House," located in Dearborn, Michigan. Kalitta's first cammer car ran well enough to qualify 4th at the 1965 U.S. Fuel & Gas Championships, at 7.65-seconds. By the spring of 1967, a full year's worth of development work paid off handsomely with a 221.12 mph top-end charge at Capitol Raceway (May 1967) and a 6.81-second qualifying shot at the U.S. Nationals at Indy. But that was just the beginning. The following winter of 1968 Kalitta built a brand new Logghe chassis AA/FD and went out and swept all three Winternationals championship events—AHRA, NHRA, and NASCAR—which was an all-time first for Kalitta, Ford, and America's fastest growing sport. Photo courtesy of Ford Photographic

This very early G.K. Callaway transparency was taken at a typical Saturday evening Top Fuel show (1964) at Fontana Drag City in Fontana, California. As you can tell from the mediocre quality, this is one of Callaway's earliest efforts. This twilight photo shows "Smokey Glen" Stokey driving the Caspary & Stokey AA/FD going up against Paul Sutherland's *Charger* in front of a packed house. Photo by G.K. Callaway

This is an early photo of Top Gas standout Bob Noice in the Noice & Pecuilli Valley Speed & Marine-sponsored AA/GD, racing Tommy Larkin at old San Fernando Raceway. Noice was one of the best in the early days of Top Gas Eliminator, but at this particular race Noice's day was done when he lit up the big red bulb. Photo by G.K. Callaway

When it came to using a variety of power plants, Top Gas was a bit more liberal and easier on parts than Top Fuel ever was. Hence, a number of Top Gas entries competed using small-block Chevrolets for power, like Northern California racer Frankie Silva and his Gateway Chevrolet-sponsored, full-bodied AA/GD, shown here in competition at Half Moon Bay, circa 1964. According to our old buddy Steve Reyes, Silva was one of the local "Valley Guys" who ran at San Jose, Vacaville, Fremont, and Half Moon Bay quite often in the Top Eliminator shows that included blown and injected gas dragsters, junior fuelers, and altereds. This was one pretty little car! Photo by G.K. Callaway

In 1965, Garden Grove, California, racers Tim "Chops" Beebe and Dave Beebe parked their Bantam-bodied Chevrolet-powered AA/FA and went Top Fuel racing with the Beebe Bros., Vinson & Sixt Chrysler-powered AA/FD. Driven by Dave and tuned by Tim, the Lee Sixt-chassis Top Fueler was a strong runner setting a low E.T. at Lions Associated Drag Strip (LADS) on October 8, 1965, with a 7.12-second clocking. On February 26, 1966, the team scored its first big win, capturing the gold at the UDRA Championships at Lions and another at the inaugural Irwindale Grand Prix. This car was also runner-up to Mike "Hawaiian" Snively in the *Hawaiian* at the 1967 U.S. Fuel & Gas Championships the following month, as well as the AHRA Springnationals held in Odessa, Texas, where the team set a top 215.82-mph record. Crowned the NHRA Division 7 Top Fuel Champion in 1966, Beebe Bros., Vinson & Sixt were runner-up in Top Fuel to "Sneaky Pete" Robinson's Ford at the NHRA World Finals held at Tulsa, Oklahoma. After Dave's exodus from the driver's seat, Tim teamed up with John "Zookeeper" Mulligan. This car eventually was re-painted two-tone candy green and re-named the *Fighting Irish*. Photo by G.K. Callaway

In the mid 1960s, La Mirada, California, fireman "Big Jim" Dunn was another altered racer who defected to the Top Fuel ranks. Shown is Dunn's first Chrysler-powered digger, which originally had been home to the very same blown small-block Chevrolet that had powered the Dunn, Merritt & Velasco Fiat AA/A. Photo by G.K. Callaway

The likeable cigar-smoking Irishman John "Zookeeper" Mulligan, from Garden Grove, California, first made a name for himself driving the Beebe Bros. & Vinson J&S Speed Center-sponsored Bantam-bodied AA/FA. Mulligan also ascended to the Top Fuel ranks about the same time the Beebes did with an assignment behind the wheel of the Adams, Wayre & Mulligan AA/FD. Mulligan immediately impressed his new partners by clocking a 219.51 at Pomona Raceway on March 24, 1966, and an even more incredible 6.95 at Carlsbad Raceway later that season on October 9. Noteworthy performances also included runner-up at the AHRA Winternationals in January 1966, the *Hot Rod* Magazine Championship Drags in June 1966, and the UDRA Las Vegas Meet on October 1, 1966. After Dave Beebe vacated the driver's seat of the Beebe Bros., Vinson & Sixt AA/FD in late 1966, and Gene Adams retired from Top Fuel racing, Mulligan teamed up with Tim "Chops" Beebe to form the team of Beebe & Mulligan. Photo by G.K. Callaway

Top Gas campaigner and supercharger builder Tommy Larkin (Larkin Blowers) is seen below charging off the Lions starting line in the summer of 1966 in his Roy Fjasted-chassis Speed Products Engineering (SPE) Top Gasser. In the late 1960s, Larkin built a new, longer wheelbase Top Gas car, which he eventually converted to fuel and raced under the "Tom and Margie Larkin" banner until the economics of the class forced his retirement in the early 1970s. Photo by G.K. Callaway

One of the most tenacious Top Gas competitors on the West Coast in the early 1960s was George Bolthoff, who basically owned the single-engine segment of the Top Gas dragster class. Bolthoff's "shift-ball" brake handle always distinguished his cars. Bolthoff is shown here in action at the 1967 *Hot Rod* Magazine Drags. Photo by G.K. Callaway

One of the teams that broke new ground in the mid 1960s was the San Diego-based "Der Wienerschnitzel" two-car Top Fuel team with Jim "Superman" Nicoll, Don "Cookie" Cook, and Leroy Goldstein alternating driving chores. In those days, nailing down a major corporate sponsor was practically unheard of for a Top Fuel car, so this was a really big deal. Performance-wise, all three team drivers knocked down the big numbers: Cook 236.37 on November 19, 1967, in Fremont, California, and Nicoll 234.00 on July 13, 1968, at Indy, as well as the following low elapsed times: Goldstein 6.71 on September 2, 1968, at Indy and Nicoll 6.17 on July 13, 1969, at U.S. 30 in Gary, Indiana. Goldstein was also runner-up at the 1968 U.S. Fuel & Gas Championships in Bakersfield, California, and at the 1968 AHRA Springnationals in Bristol, Tennessee, before accepting an assignment driving the Ramchargers AA/FD. One vivid drag racing memory I have of team "Der Wienerschnitzel" was that they used to pass out small water decals of the Der Wienerschnitzel Top Fuel dragster to all their fans. Today, these decals are worth their weight in gold to serious drag racing memorabilia collectors.

The first ever PDA Championships were held at Lions Associated Drag Strip (LADS) on July 20, 1967. In this photo, Don "Snake" Prudhomme blasts off the Lions starting line in the newly full bodied Baney, Pink & Prudhomme *Brand Motors Ford Special* AA/FD, which was hot off winning Top Fuel Eliminator at the 1967 NHRA Springnationals at Bristol, Tennessee. Powered by one of the new 427 SOHC Ford engines, which was considered a breath of fresh air in Top Fuel racing, the Brand Motors Ford Special AA/FD held its own against the Chryslers. In fact, Prudhomme handily won that first PDA event at Lions, defeating Beebe & Mulligan's *Fighting Irish* AA/FD on the final, clocking a 7.29-212.26 to a smoked-in 7.92-158.45. However, by the end of the 1968 drag racing season, Prudhomme was out of the hot seat and "Hollywood Kelly" Brown took over the controls. The reasons why Prudhomme quit driving the Brand Motors car were twofold. One was that the 427 SOHC Ford cars exhibited a rather nasty habit of oiling down the driver, which Prudhomme had grown tired of; and the other was that Chrysler Western Region public relations representative Jack McFarland made Prudhomme a sweet factory deal, racing under the Chrysler-Plymouth banner. So, it was on to greener (or at least less oily) pastures for Prudhomme. Photo by G.K. Callaway

In the spring of 1967, Larry Dixon Sr. parked his *Fireside Inn* AA/FMR and stepped into the driver's seat of Darryl Greenameyer's Dave Zeuschel-engine *Smirnoff Special*. Of course, Greenameyer also owned the *Miss Smirnoff* Unlimited Hydroplane, which in those days was quite competitive in offshore boat racing. The *Smirnoff Special* was as quick as it was beautiful, setting Low E.T. of the Meet at 7.01 at PDA in 1967. Unfortunately, budget cutbacks in Greenameyer's racing program ultimately forced the team to disband. Photo by G.K. Callaway

Here's a nice shot of the Rapp, Rossi & Muldanado *Purple Gang* AA/FD with future land-speed record holder Gary Gabelich behind the wheel hazing the tires of the Lions Associated Drag Strip starting line in the summer of 1967. Industry veteran Ronnie Rapp was considered the spark plug of the operation. When he wasn't building Top Fuel Chrysler engines, Rapp did stints as a general manager at both Ansen Industries and Doug's Headers in the late 1960s. Of course, RR&M's favorite color was purple, hence the nickname *Purple Gang*. At the local Top Fuel shows Rapp, Rossi, Muldanado and Gabelich could always be counted on to knock down the big numbers. Photo by G.K. Callaway

In this G.K. Callaway photo taken at the inaugural PDA romp at Lions Associated Drag Strip, Dave Beebe in the Beebe Bros., Vinson & Sixt AA/FD is out on Jeep Hampshire driving the Caspary, Stokey & Hampshire AA/FD. Most likely, this was the second or third round of action, as it's obviously late in the day. Check out that crowd! Photo by G.K. Callaway

By the mid 1960s, Top Fuel cars had taken on their own personalities with full-bodied coachwork and lots of color. A case in point is the Bobby Hightower-driven *Cow Palace Shell* AA/FD owned by South San Francisco's Jesse Perkins. Photographer G.K. Callaway caught Hightower blasting off the Lions Associated Drag Strip starting line one late Saturday afternoon. Check out those awesome header flames! Photo by G.K. Callaway

Perennial Top Gas favorite Bob Noice (Noice & Pecuilli) is seen going up against Billy "Kid" Scott, who was driving the Adams & Rasmussen-Beacon Auto Parts AA/GD at the U.S. Pro Dragster Championships during the summer of 1967 at Lions Associated Drag Strip (LADS). Noice & Pecuilli put this car together strictly for this race (which Noice would ultimately lose to Scott), using one of Sonny Diaz' Top Gas Chrysler engines. Anyone who ever went to a dragster race at Lions and sat in the push-road bleachers never forgets the sights, smells, and sounds that were distinctively Lions. These folks would end up covered with "Goodyear freckles," those little black bits of tire rubber that sprinkle on your face and everywhere else, and are no fun to wash out. Photo by G.K. Callaway

This photo shows Hank Westmorland behind the wheel of Don "The Beachcomber" Johnson's Speed Products Engineering-chassis (SPE), Ed Pink Chrysler engine AA/FD during weekend Top Fuel action at OCIR. The year began with the team embarking on a somewhat lucrative national tour, with one of the highlights being a Top Fuel win at the 1969 NHRA Springnationals held at the newly opened Dallas Motor Speedway complex in Carrollton, Texas. Johnson-Westmorland clocked a 6.84-214.79 to defeat Lou Baney's *Brand Motors Ford Special* entry with newly installed driver "Hollywood Kelly" Brown behind the wheel. Brown carded a losing 6.91-184.00. Photo by G.K. Callaway

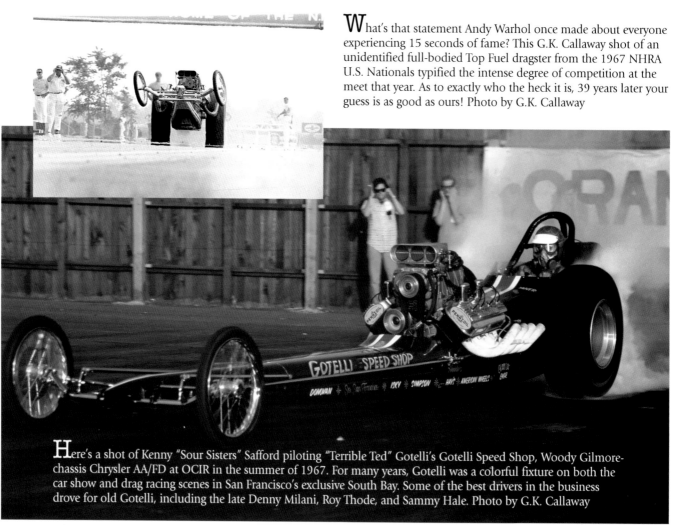

What's that statement Andy Warhol once made about everyone experiencing 15 seconds of fame? This G.K. Callaway shot of an unidentified full-bodied Top Fuel dragster from the 1967 NHRA U.S. Nationals typified the intense degree of competition at the meet that year. As to exactly who the heck it is, 39 years later your guess is as good as ours! Photo by G.K. Callaway

Here's a shot of Kenny "Sour Sisters" Safford piloting "Terrible Ted" Gotelli's Gotelli Speed Shop, Woody Gilmore-chassis Chrysler AA/FD at OCIR in the summer of 1967. For many years, Gotelli was a colorful fixture on both the car show and drag racing scenes in San Francisco's exclusive South Bay. Some of the best drivers in the business drove for old Gotelli, including the late Denny Milani, Roy Thode, and Sammy Hale. Photo by G.K. Callaway

The San Diego-based Top Gas team of Steiner & Stebbins rarely ventured outside the Golden State with their late-model Hemi-engine Top Gas car. But then, the allure of the U.S. Nationals at Indianapolis Raceway Park always brought out the hopefuls in an attempt to become the best the sport had to offer. Photo by G.K. Callaway

Good tires always seemed to be the key problem in getting the twin-engine Top Gas cars to hook up. In 1968, the amazing twin-engine *Freight Train* AA/GD owned by John Peters finally found those much-desired Goodyear tires, and in spite of numerous driver changes, ran over the competition throughout the entire season, recording a best of 7.30-207.00 with drivers Roy "Goob" Tuller, Bob "Floyd Lippencote Jr." Muravez, and Billy "Kid" Scott taking turns behind the tiller. Lippencote's finest hour was winning the Hot Rod Championship Drag Races (shown here) in June 1968 at Riverside International Raceway. This train has since been restored, and when it isn't on display at the Wally Parks NHRA Motorsports Museum, it's frequently displayed on the drag racing nostalgia circuit. Photo by G.K. Callaway

John "Zookeeper" Mulligan was known as one of the "Garden Grove Gang" and was chauffer for teams like Adams, Wayre & Mulligan, Adams & Mulligan, and the Beebe & Mulligan "Fighting Irish" AA/FDs. After brother Dave Beebe vacated the driver's seat of the Beebe Bros., Vinson & Sixt AA/FD in 1967, (prior to driving Funny Cars Dave briefly drove for Tony Waters), John Mulligan jumped behind the wheel and started making drag racing history. In 1967, the team, now known as the Fighting Irish, broke the elapsed time record at OCIR and Lions Associated Drag Strip (LADS), 6.79-seconds on October 7, 1967, and 6.71-seconds on October 21, 1967, respectively, as well as setting the Top MPH record that same day at Lions, at 230.76. That year, Beebe & Mulligan also finished in the runner-up spot at the inaugural PDA Championships to Baney, Pink & Prudhomme at Lions, running a tire-smoking 7.92-158.45. In 1968, Beebe & Mulligan continued knocking down the big numbers, setting Top Speed and Low E.T. at the AHRA Springnationals on May 7, 1968, in Bristol, Tennessee, with 6.85-226.60, which was also the first six-second run in AHRA national event history. Then came a 232.55 top-end charge at Englishtown on May 30, 1968, followed by a 233.76 at Indy on September 2, 1968. E.T. records that year include a 6.65 on June 16, 1968, in Englishtown, and back-to-back 6.66s at Detroit on August 10, 1968, and Gary, Indiana, on August 11, 1968. That year the Fighting Irish would also be runner-up at the 1968 NHRA Springnationals against "Big Daddy" Don Garlits and at the NHRA World Finals, racing against Bennie "Wizard" Osborn.

In the winter of 1968, famed car builder and international road racing champion Carroll Hall Shelby briefly went Top Fuel racing, sponsoring the Baney, Pink & Prudhomme Brand Motors Ford Special, which was aptly re-named *Shelby's Super Snake*. Actually, the deal was more for publicity than anything else, with both Ford and Goodyear (Shelby is Goodyear's number one racing tire distributor) obviously pulling the strings. Shown in this photo are Shelby (left), "Miss Winternationals" and B-movie queen Celeste Yarnall, and Don "Snake" Prudhomme.

In the summer of 1968, the Fighting Irish debuted an all-new Woody Gilmore Top Fuel car and immediately ran 6.70-230.00 at the PDA race at OCIR. The following February also produced a Top Fuel win at the 1969 NHRA Winternationals, where they recorded a 6.95-226.00 over Don "Snake" Prudhomme. However, the strain of running all those big numbers was beginning to take its toll on Tim "Chops" Beebe's venerable 392 Chrysler Hemi engines, as witnessed in this photo of B&M kicking a connecting rod out during a night race at OCIR. Shortly thereafter, Beebe & Mulligan switched over to a late-model Chrysler Hemi and immediately continued their winning form. Notable performances included a 231.50 on May 30, 1969, at Martin, Michigan, and a 233.32 top-end charge on June 16, 1969, at the Hot Rod Drags at Riverside, California. Wins included a two-day sweep at the Olympics of Drag Racing at Union Grove, Wisconsin, as well as winning Top Fuel at the New York National Speedway Smoker's Meet, setting both Top Speed (228.42) and Low E.T. at 6.63-seconds. The team's last great performance was setting Low E.T. of the Meet (6.43-seconds) at Indy on September 1, 1969. Unfortunately, a horrendous engine fire and crash while racing "T.V. Tommy" Ivo (round one) that same weekend at Indy cost John "Zookeeper" Mulligan his life. After spending several weeks in the hospital, Mulligan passed away from complications from pneumonia, and drag racing lost one of the best there ever was.

In 1968–'69, Top Gas standout Bob Noice experienced two of the best years of his racing career. He first beat the team of Bill Schultz and Gerry Glenn to annex the NHRA Division 7 Top Gas crown, as shown in this photo taken at Irwindale Raceway's WWCS finale. In 1969, the team of Noice & Pecuilli ventured to the NHRA World Finals in Tulsa, Oklahoma, where they defeated Rockford, Illinois' Mark Pieri to capture the NHRA Top Gas World Championship, running a 7.83-195.00 to Pieri's losing 7.87-188.00. Photo by G.K. Callaway

This publicity photo was taken of Don "Snake" Prudhomme and "Miss *Hot Rod* Magazine Drags" just prior to Prudhomme's participation in the 1969 event of the same name, held on the one mile straightaway at the now defunct Riverside International Raceway facility. At that final HRM Championship Drags event, Prudhomme's new Plymouth-powered, Keith Black-engine *Wynn's Winder* went out in the semis, losing to 1968 winner Steve "Mandrill" Carbone. Photos by G.K. Callaway & Bob McClurg

The 1969 *Hot Rod* Magazine Championship Drag Races was also where these photos of "Big Daddy" Don Garlits and his *Smothers Bros./Wynn's Charger* (aka *Swamp Rat XII-C*) were captured in action. In 1969, racing fan Dickie Smothers sponsored his own Smother's Brothers Comedy Hour racing team, which consisted of a fleet of Oldsmobile Stock Eliminator cars and two Top Fuel cars, one belonging to Garlits and the other belonging to "Beach Boy Jim" Busby. Predictably, Garlits' *SR XII-C* was quite successful, winning the PDA Championship, a three-event Top Fuel Trifecta that included the likes of Garlits, Don "Snake" Prudhomme, James Warren, "Captain Chris" Karamesines, Jerry "King" Ruth, Tom "Mongoose" McEwen, Creitz & Carbone, and Beebe & Mulligan. PDA's Top Fuel Attrition Race started November 9, 1968 at Lions Associated Drag Strip, where Garlits won. Then it went to San Diego County's Carlsbad Raceway the next day, where Garlits also triumphed, effectively tying up the series. They again raced at the Sacramento River Delta Region's Sacramento Raceway on November 17, 1968, where James Warren won the final foray. Other wins for *SR XII-C* that year included a Top Fuel win at the Sears Point National Open in March 1969, as well as finishing up in the semifinal round at the *Hot Rod* Magazine Championship Drags, where Garlits lost to eventual winner Larry Dixon driving the *Howard's Cams Rattler*. Prior to being sold as a display car to Wynn's of Belgium, where *SR XII-C* remained until 1984, the sport's longest full-bodied, front-engine Top Fuel car (215 inches) ran a career best of 6.80-240.00. Photos by Bob McClurg & G.K. Callaway

These photos of Dwight Salisbury in the "Beach Boy Jim" Busby-owned *Smothers Brothers Beach Boys Special* were taken at the 1969 HRM Drags at Riverside Raceway. The *Smothers Brothers Beach Boys Special* was the second half of comedian Dickie Smothers' Top Fuel assault team for 1969. However, the Beach Boys' Top Fuel car differed significantly from "Big Daddy" Don Garlits' *SR XII-C*. Busby's car featured a Roy Fjasted-Speed Products Engineering (SPE) chassis, which was a bit sleeker and featured a considerably shorter wheelbase. A blown 392 early Chrysler Hemi instead of a late-model "Elephant Motor" powered the car.

Busby's car started out the 1969 season by winning Best Appearing Car at the NHRA Winternationals at Pomona, California, while tying for Top Speed of the Meet honors (229.00) along with Dick Whitted, Jack Ewell, Bell & Olson, and event winner John "Zookeeper" Mulligan. On May 25, 1969, the team also set a new E.T. record at U.S. 30 in Gary, Indiana, at 6.48-seconds. However, like the original Surfers Top Fuel team, the cold, hard economic realities of competing in Top Fuel eventually brought about the team's demise. Both Busby and Salisbury continued racing, however. Salisbury campaigned his own rear-engine Top Fuel car named *Salisbury's Stake*, and Busby experimented with a number of different road race and drag race car projects (like Busby's twin-engine DOHC Ford-engine Top Fuel car) well into the 1970s. Photos by Bob McClurg & G.K. Callaway

In 2006, we lost one of drag racing's most talented and colorful Top Fuel drivers with the sudden passing of Steve "Mandrill" Carbone, who first emerged in the early 1960s driving dragsters for AHRA campaigner and lifelong friend, Tulsa, Oklahoma's Bob Creitz. Commissioned as a mate in the "Greek Fleet," an honor bestowed to only the most tenacious Top Fuel handlers on the AHRA circuit by none other than "Captain Chris" Karamesines himself, Carbone nonetheless distinguished himself in both NHRA and AHRA national event competition in equal proportions.

In June 1968, Steve won Top Fuel Eliminator at the *Hot Rod* Magazine Championship Drag Races driving John Bateman's *Atlas Oil Tool Special*, triumphing over "Hollywood Kelly" Brown in the Dean Engineering car. To this day, they're still talking about the huge victory party and ensuing melee that occurred at Downey, California's Tahitian Village the following weekend. Other accomplishments included winning the 1968 PDA Meet at Fremont, California, driving the Creitz & Donovan car, and finishing in the runner-up spot to "Big Daddy" Don Garlits at Indy 1968.

The following season, Carbone finished in the runner-up position at OCIR's 1969 PDA event to Larry Dixon's *Howard Cams Rattler* while winning the 1969 *Popular Hot Rodding* Magazine Championships at Martin, Michigan, over Powers & Riley. Carbone also set Top Speed of the Meet at the AHRA Springnationals in Bob Creitz's car at 217.38 and ran 6.54-seconds in competition at Indy 1969. Carbone also won the 1969 AHRA Points Finale at Tulsa. For the 1970 season, Carbone briefly drove for Larry "Soapy Sales" Huff, winning the NHRA World Finals at Dallas. Then he went out on his own, fielding a late-model-powered Don Long-chassis AA/FD, and that car was the subject of a race that everybody still talks about—the "Great Burn-Down of 1971!"

In spite of Carbone's very respectable 6.39-second qualifying number at Indianapolis 1971, everybody was talking about Garlits and his revolutionary *Swamp Rat XIV* mid-engine dragster, which had been progressively mowing down the competition round by round. At that event, Carbone was likewise working his way through the field and met

Garlits in the final. Remembering that Garlits had played the old burn-down game at the 1968 event just two years before, Carbone refused to stage first. Both cars sat pre-staged with engines smoking and header flames belching for what seemed like an eternity. But neither would light the staged bulb. Of course, this totally infuriated former NHRA Chief Starter Eddie "Buster" Couch, who finally had had enough. Couch flicked the "race" button on his Chrondek remote control box and backed away. The minute Carbone's black dragster crept into the staging beams, the Christmas tree cycled into automatic countdown, and Carbone was gone! Steve clocked a 6.48-229.00 to Garlits' up-in-smoke 6.65-229.00. It would be the last major NHRA national event win for a front-engine Top Fuel car.

Just prior to his retirement in late 1972, Carbone showed that he still had what it took, winning Top Fuel Eliminator over shipmate Jim "Superman" Nicoll at the AHRA Winternationals in Phoenix. For the remainder of his life, Carbone concentrated on building everything from sprint car engines, to engines for bracket cars, and street rods at his Tulsa race shop, Steve Carbone Racing Engines. Photos by Bob McClurg and G.K. Callaway

In 1970, Larry Dixon Sr. and his wife, Pat, campaigned this beautiful candy blue Speed Products Engineering (SPE) Ed Pink-motivated front engine AA/FD. This classic night shot racing Gary "Mr. C" Cochran at OCIR tells the whole story—header flames, nitro fumes, and intense concentration. That year, Dixon's biggest win came at the NHRA Winternationals in Pomona, California, where he defeated Tony "Loner" Nancy in the final round. The following year, Dixon also set Low E.T. at Bakersfield with a 6.64-second shot, as well as taking the runner-up spot at the 1971 Irwindale Grand Prix, where Dixon set Top Speed (227.84) and Low E.T. at 6.49 seconds. Dixon went on to drive the Chevrolet-powered *Howard's Cams Rat* rear-engine digger for Rod Dunne (Dixon-Dunne), which became the first Top Fuel Chevrolet in the 5s.

This front-engine Top Fuel blow-over by Walnut Creek, California, chassis builder and 1970 NHRA Division 7 Top Fuel champ Jim Davis was the second of its kind recorded in national event history. I took this from-the-hip grab shot during qualifying at the 1971 March Meet in Bakersfield, California. Notice that NHRA photographer Leslie Lovett (who is holding a Hasselblad medium format camera with a 500-mm telephoto lens) is just standing helplessly by as Davis bowls 'er over. Fortunately, other than a bruised ego, Davis escaped injury.

Gary "Mr. C" Cochran, the Fountain Valley, California, Top Gas racer-turned Top Fuel campaigner and Larry Dixon's opponent in the photo above, was one of the very best on the starting lights. Cochran was also one of the finest mechanics in the business, and regardless of the fact that he had to do everything on a very tight budget, he could always be counted on to make a respectable showing. Aside from winning a ton of local events, which included Top Fuel at Lions Associated Drag Strip 1969 AHRA Grand American, Cochran also toured, albeit on a limited basis. On-the-road wins included capturing the Top Fuel crown at Union Grove, Wisconsin's 1972 Olympics of Drag Racing event. This photo of Cochran was taken off the earthen berm at OCIR in the summer of 1970.

"Big Daddy" Don Garlits gyrates off the Indy starting line on a qualifying pass at the 1970 U.S. Nationals in *Swamp Rat XIII*. SR-XIII ran a best of 6.50-seconds at Gainesville in February, and 232.00 at U.S. 30 in Gary, Indiana, in August 1970. Official NHRA Starter Eddie "Buster" Couch is seen in the background. This was the same car that was cut in half when a transmission exploded later that year at the Lions Associated Drag Strip AHRA Grand American race. Photo By G.K. Callaway

Northern California racer Dennis Baca in the Baca & Freels AA/FD grabs some air coming off the starting line at Lions Associated Drag Strip in the summer of 1970. Perhaps Dennis Baca's biggest claim to fame was that he won the NHRA Division 7 Top Fuel Championship in 1971, in spite of the fact that he never really knocked down any major event wins with his front-engine fuel car. However, Baca did fare a little better with his rear engine cars. Today, Dennis' son David carries on the Baca family tradition in NHRA-POWERade Top Fuel competition. Photo by G.K. Callaway

This is "Captain Billy" Tidwell driving "Kool Mike" Kuhl's Woody Gilmore-chassis AA/FD during PDA qualifying at OCIR. Although this team didn't last that long, the team set Low E.T. (6.72-second) at the AHRA Grand American Championships at Lions Associated Drag Strip June 21–22, 1969. After that, Carl Olsen assumed the controls, and the Top Fuel team of Kuhl & Olson went on to become one of the premier teams in the sport.

In the late 1960s I was able to vicariously live out my life-long fantasy of owning and/or driving a Top Fuel dragster through my older cousin Bill Hansen from Mt. Vernon, New York. For a couple of years, my uncle Victor McClurg kept telling me about a dragster that my cousin Bill had been racing. Of course, when I pressed my uncle about what kind of dragster it was, I would always get the same answer. "How the hell do I know? It's a dragster!" Eventually I got to visit my cousin, in the summer of 1971, and couldn't believe my eyes when he opened the door of his one-car garage. There sat a B&L Engines fuel-burning 392 Hemi-powered Woody Gilmore car! From 1969 to 1971, Hansen and his partner Louis Ferrante had been campaigning the *Eastwind* AA/FD in NHRA's Northeast Division 1 (a.k.a., Land of NED) with moderate success, clocking a best of 6.79-227.00. Unfortunately, a lack of finances kept the guys from getting too far, but old cousin Bill's moment in the sun came during the first round of Top Fuel eliminations at the 1971 NHRA Summernationals at Raceway Park in Englishtown, where he strapped a holeshot on none other than Tom "Mongoose" McEwen and never looked back!

In 1971, Mattel Hot Wheels designed a pair of goofy looking square dragster bodies for both Wildlife Racing's Tom "Mongoose" McEwen and Don "Snake" Prudhomme's front-engine Top Fuel cars. Everybody in drag racing, Prudhomme and McEwen included, thought the cars were strange-looking. Of the two, McEwen actually drove his car more than Prudhomme did, but the truth of the matter was that the team's Plymouth-bodied Mattel Hot Wheels Funny Cars were infinitely more popular with the fans. Here we see McEwen flashing the victory sign at the 1971 Bakersfield March Meet. That's veteran drag racing photographer Alan Earman standing in the background.

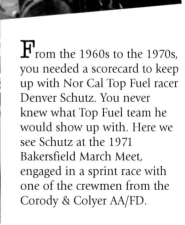

From the 1960s to the 1970s, you needed a scorecard to keep up with Nor Cal Top Fuel racer Denver Schutz. You never knew what Top Fuel team he would show up with. Here we see Schutz at the 1971 Bakersfield March Meet, engaged in a sprint race with one of the crewmen from the Corody & Colyer AA/FD.

This overhead view of Austin Myers in the (Butch) Hummel & Myers twin Chrysler engine AA/GD was taken from the "buzzard perch" on top of the Hurst Performance crossover bridge at Indianapolis Raceway Park during Top Gas qualifying at the 1971 NHRA U.S. Nationals. Of course, that was the last year for Top Gas, and a lot of people were sorry to see the blackey carbons (especially these twin-engine behemoths) fall by the wayside.

Here's Preston Davis behind the wheel of Raymond Godman's *Tennessee Bo Weevil* AA/FD at Indy 1970. Of course, you could always tell it was Godman's car pulling up to the line because it sported a rebel flag on top of the roll cage. These guys generally ran well, and although national event wins were few and far between, they captured both the 1968 and 1970 NHRA Division 3 Top Fuel Championships, as well as setting Top Speed of the Meet on September 28, 1968, at the AHRA U.S. Open in Rockingham, North Carolina. Along the way they were also runner-up to Mooneyham & Martini at the 1971 IHRA Springnationals in Bristol, Tennessee. In the early 1970s, Godman & Davis went Funny Car racing for a while prior to pulling the plug around 1976.

This rather unconventional shot of "T.V. Tommy" Ivo was taken at Union Grove, Wisconsin's 1970 Olympics of Drag Racing event. Judging from the look of the tires, it's apparent that old Ivo has himself a "one-legger." In laymen's terms, that means there's something wrong with the positraction unit in the rear end. This Hanna-bodied Woody Gilmore car was Ivo's last front-engine dragster before moving to rear-engine Top Fuel cars. Performances included a 6.56 clocking at York, Pennsylvania, on April 26, 1969.

This shot of Jim Paoli's "Big Daddy" Don Garlits-chassis *Yankee Packrat* AA/FD was taken from the roof of the Gainesville Raceway tower during 1971 NHRA Gatornationals Top Fuel qualifying. Jim Paoli's racing operation was what you would call a family effort, as his likeable mother and father (whom all the racers called Mom and Pop) always accompanied him to the races. No slouch in the performance department, Paoli's *Yankee Packrat* won both the 1970 and 1971 NHRA Division 3 Top Fuel titles. Paoli was the 1971 United Drag Racers Association (UDRA) Top Fuel Champion, and he also ran the IHRA circuit with this car, although we know of no big wins to his credit. In 1972, Paoli traded in his Top Fueler for a Chevrolet Vega Funny Car that he campaigned with moderate success.

One of my favorite Top Fuel cars was Jim and Allison Lee's early Chrysler-powered *Great Expectations* AA/FD, from The Plains, Virginia. For more than a decade, the Lees competed in both NHRA Division 1 and at the national event level with a number of top-notch drivers including Hank Westmorland, Bub Reese, and Tom Raley. Performances included winning the NHRA Division 1 Northeast Division Championship in 1967 (Westmorland); the 1969 and 1970 Northeast Division Championships (Raley); and running a 6.51 at Indy on September 1, 1969, a 6.56 at Atco, New Jersey, on September 7, 1969, and a 6.53 on October 25, 1969, at Dallas.

Probably the very last guy in the known universe to campaign a front-engine Top Fuel car (1974) was Jack Mitchell from the Rockford, Illinois, Top Fuel team of Mitchell, Hay & Klentz. This car was absolutely awesome with its killer burnouts and huge top-end charges. Of course, by 1975 Mitchell and company were also running a rear-engine car.

RIGHT INSET: Carl Casper's *Young American* AA/FD was one of the last top-flight front-engine dragsters to originate out of Keith Black's South Gate, California, engine shop. Driven by Hawaiian-born handler Danny "On The Gas" Ongias, the *Young American* was a strong runner, carding performances like a 6.49 at Indy on September 7, 1970, and a 6.51 on October 24, 1970, at Lions Associated Drag Strip. However, the *Young American* Top Fuel car distinguished itself more for what actually happened to it away from the drag strip. One dark night, a band of thugs broke into Black's shop and stole the entire rig, race car, trailer, spares—the whole shebang! Rumors and innuendo abounded. However, no one knew of the car's whereabouts. That is, until the Brotherhood of (L.A.) Street Racers' "Big Willie" Robinson stepped in and assisted Casper and the local authorities (through the use of Robinson's extensive underground network) in recovering everything, right down to the last nut and bolt! Photo by G.K. Callaway

Here's further proof that drag racing is hereditary. This is the team of Mooneyham & Martini in Top Fuel at the 1971 IHRA Springnationals held at Bristol, Tennessee, in June 1971. If the name Mooneyham sounds familiar, it's because Fred Mooneyham is the son of the famed blower builder and engine tuner Gene Mooneyham of "554" fuel coupe fame. These guys were some of the last of the front-engine Top Fuel holdouts.

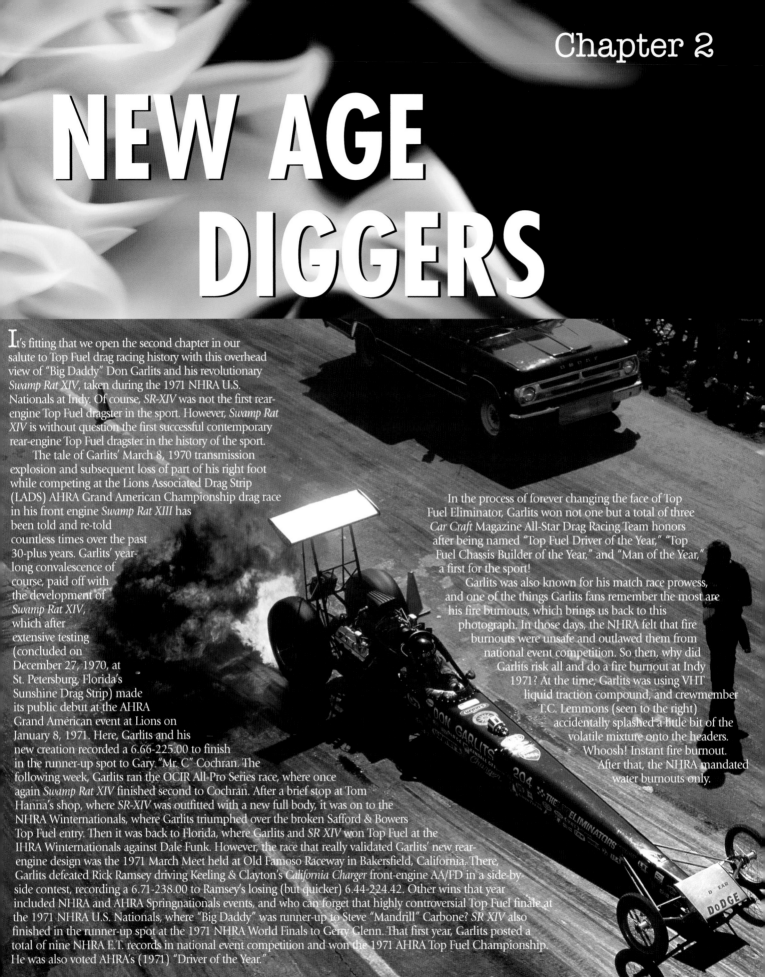

Chapter 2

NEW AGE DIGGERS

It's fitting that we open the second chapter in our salute to Top Fuel drag racing history with this overhead view of "Big Daddy" Don Garlits and his revolutionary *Swamp Rat XIV*, taken during the 1971 NHRA U.S. Nationals at Indy. Of course, *SR-XIV* was not the first rear-engine Top Fuel dragster in the sport. However, *Swamp Rat XIV* is without question the first successful contemporary rear-engine Top Fuel dragster in the history of the sport.

The tale of Garlits' March 8, 1970 transmission explosion and subsequent loss of part of his right foot while competing at the Lions Associated Drag Strip (LADS) AHRA Grand American Championship drag race in his front engine *Swamp Rat XIII* has been told and re-told countless times over the past 30-plus years. Garlits' year-long convalescence of course, paid off with the development of *Swamp Rat XIV*, which after extensive testing (concluded on December 27, 1970, at St. Petersburg, Florida's Sunshine Drag Strip) made its public debut at the AHRA Grand American event at Lions on January 8, 1971. Here, Garlits and his new creation recorded a 6.66-225.00 to finish in the runner-up spot to Gary "Mr. C" Cochran. The following week, Garlits ran the OCIR All-Pro Series race, where once again *Swamp Rat XIV* finished second to Cochran. After a brief stop at Tom Hanna's shop, where *SR-XIV* was outfitted with a new full body, it was on to the NHRA Winternationals, where Garlits triumphed over the broken Safford & Bowers Top Fuel entry. Then it was back to Florida, where Garlits and *SR XIV* won Top Fuel at the IHRA Winternationals against Dale Funk. However, the race that really validated Garlits' new rear-engine design was the 1971 March Meet held at Old Famoso Raceway in Bakersfield, California. There, Garlits defeated Rick Ramsey driving Keeling & Clayton's *California Charger* front-engine AA/FD in a side-by-side contest, recording a 6.71-238.00 to Ramsey's losing (but quicker) 6.44-224.42. Other wins that year included NHRA and AHRA Springnationals events, and who can forget that highly controversial Top Fuel finale at the 1971 NHRA U.S. Nationals, where "Big Daddy" was runner-up to Steve "Mandrill" Carbone? *SR XIV* also finished in the runner-up spot at the 1971 NHRA World Finals to Gerry Glenn. That first year, Garlits posted a total of nine NHRA E.T. records in national event competition and won the 1971 AHRA Top Fuel Championship. He was also voted AHRA's (1971) "Driver of the Year."

In the process of forever changing the face of Top Fuel Eliminator, Garlits won not one but a total of three *Car Craft* Magazine All-Star Drag Racing Team honors after being named "Top Fuel Driver of the Year," "Top Fuel Chassis Builder of the Year," and "Man of the Year," a first for the sport!

Garlits was also known for his match race prowess, and one of the things Garlits fans remember the most are his fire burnouts, which brings us back to this photograph. In those days, the NHRA felt that fire burnouts were unsafe and outlawed them from national event competition. So then, why did Garlits risk all and do a fire burnout at Indy 1971? At the time, Garlits was using VHT liquid traction compound, and crewmember T.C. Lemmons (seen to the right) accidentally splashed a little bit of the volatile mixture onto the headers. Whoosh! Instant fire burnout. After that, the NHRA mandated water burnouts only.

"Big Daddy" Don Garlits' runaway success with *SR-XIV* prompted others to jump on the rear-engine Top Fuel bandwagon. In 1972, NHRA Division 2 Top Fuel driver Clayton Harris drove Jack MacKay's New Dimension Homes-sponsored AA/FD to the NHRA Southeast Division 2 Top Fuel title, along with winning the *Popular Hot Rodding* Magazine Championships at Martin, Michigan, proving that Garlits and *SR-XIV* could be beaten in national event competition by another rear-engine dragster. Harris also finished in the runner-up position to Garlits at the IHRA Winternationals in Lakeland, Florida, posting a 7.03-221.67 that year, along with a runner-up finish to Jim Walther at the 1972 NHRA World Finals. Harris also set Low E.T. of the Meet (6.07) at Miami, and Top Speed of the Meet at the IHRA Winternationals in Lakeland, at 227.27. At the 1972 U.S. Nationals at Indy, Harris also peeled off a 234.98, and a month later a 230.17 at the NHRA World Finals in Ontario, Canada, where this picture was taken. Financial troubles forced the Harris & MacKay team to disband at the close of the 1972 drag racing season. However, Harris continued racing by himself and in fact defended his NHRA Division 2 Top Fuel crown the following season. One of the things that has always intrigued this writer about Harris & MacKay's *New Dimension* rear-engine Top Fuel car is that it ran all those big numbers without the benefit of a rear wing. With minimal downforce, that must have been one hairy ride!

The legendary NHRA Division 7 Top Fuel team of "California Carl" Olson and "Kool Mike" Kuhl (Kuhl & Olson) got together in the late 1960s and were a force to be reckoned with for nearly a decade. Once the team stepped up to a new Woody Gilmore rear-engine car in late 1971, K&O were off and running. Some of Kuhl & Olson's more noteworthy accomplishments included carding a 6.09 on December 2, 1972, at the Lions Associated Drag Strip Grand Premiere event, winning Top Fuel at the 1972 NHRA Winternationals, finishing in the runner-up position to Tom "Mongoose" McEwen at the 1972 Bakersfield March Meet, and finishing in the runner-up spot in Top Fuel to Chip Woodall at the 1972 NHRA Springnationals in June 1972. K&O also won the 1972 IHRA Longhorn Nationals in a somewhat dubious manner. A clutch explosion cut the car in half *after* the finish line lights, but fortunately Olson was able to keep the front half of the digger upright and off the guardrail. After that race, K&O took possession of a brand new long-wheelbase Woody Gilmore car. The old car was repaired and sold to European Top Fuel racer Clive Skilton, and it competed at the 1973 NHRA Winternationals racing under Team Castrol colors. Then, the digger was shipped home to the U.K., where it became European drag racing's first successful rear-engine AA/FD. Of course, Olson eventually went to work for NHRA and later the FIA. Kuhl became one of the top supercharger rebuilders (Kuhl Superchargers) in the country. In recent years, Kuhl has restored K&O's old front-engine Woody Gilmore car and whenever possible, he and Carl participate in the Good Guys and California Hot Rod Reunion Cacklefests.

In 1971, Southern California automotive artists John "Waldo" Glaspy and Jim Moser built this Can Am-style Top Fuel streamliner and went drag racing. Based on a conventional Jim Davis rear-engine dragster chassis, and powered by a Donovan (417) Chrysler Hemi, the Boraxo streamliner featured a Glaspy-designed, one-piece fiberglass, reverse tilting body painted by "Wild Bill" Carter and personally lettered by Glaspy and Moser. Although the car was meant to compete in Top Fuel, mechanical problems kept it from ever making a full pass. However, once converted over to alcohol, the 'liner ran a best of 7.19-199.00 at OCIR. Drivers included Dwight Salisbury, Moser, and Roger Gates. Of course, a lack of finances kept the Boraxo car from ever realizing its true performance potential, and years later Glaspy's father ended up trading the car for some property in Arkansas. However, we've recently heard reports that Glaspy and Moser's Boraxo streamliner has been seen for sale at a number of your higher-profile automotive swap meets around the country. In spite of the fact that the 'liner has been making the rounds, there have been no takers.

Largo, Florida's "Starvin' Marvin" Schwartz was Pinellas County's answer to "Big Daddy" Don Garlits. But the reality was that on many occasions throughout Schwartz's storied career he would often team up with Garlits driving one of Garlits' cars. Schwartz began drag racing back in the 1950s, in a time when mechanical skills were far more important to running a successful Top Fuel car than money was, and Schwartz became renown as the ultimate "bucks down" fuel racer. Hence, the nickname "Starvin' Marvin."

"Those were the days when all you needed to do was go to the junkyard and pull a 392 Hemi out of an old Chrysler 300, bolt on a blower, drop in some nitro, and go racing," said longtime Schwartz cohort Al Sedita.

"Yeah, that purple stuff sure made it go fast. Well, at least once," said Schwartz's childhood friend John Ballard.

Of course, the likeable Schwartz was best remembered for finishing second overall to

Garlits at the 1965 U.S. Fuel & Gas Championships at Bakersfield, driving the *Garlits Chassis Special*. In 1970, Schwartz also pinch-hit, fulfilling Garlits' booking engagements driving the repaired *Swamp Rat XIII* during Garlits' lengthy convalescence.

On his own Schwartz won numerous Top Fuel titles, including the 1973 IHRA Springnationals event at Bristol, Tennessee. Schwartz was also runner-up to Garlits at the 1973 PDA National Challenge in Tulsa, Oklahoma, campaigning one of the four customer cars built from Garlits' phenomenally successful *Swamp Rat XIV* chassis jig. The car ran a career best of 5.84-242.00. Sadly, Schwartz lost his life competing at the 1980 AHRA Winternationals in Tuscon, Arizona. In 1999, Schwartz was posthumously inducted into the Don Garlits Drag Racing Museum Hall of Fame, with John Ballard accepting the honors.

Cincinnati, Ohio, racer Jim Bucher, the winner of the last NHRA Top Gas Eliminator title at the 1972 NHRA Mattel Hot Wheels Supernationals, driving his *Kenner SSP* twin-engine small-block Chevrolet AA/GD, took the "less is better" approach when building his big-block Chevrolet-powered Top Fuel car in 1973. This machine weighed in at a scant 1,100 pounds, and it clocked a best of 6.079-seconds at Gainesville. It also set Low E.T. of the Meet at Indy that same year during qualifying with a 6.09, ahead of event winner Gary Beck. And that was with a nitro-burning Chevrolet! That same year, Bucher's Chevy was runner-up to Beck at the *Popular Hot Rodding* Magazine Championships located in Martin, Michigan. Unfortunately, Bucher lost a fight against cancer a year or so later. Had that not happened, he might have been the first Top Fuel Chevrolet in the 5s. Today, Bucher's amazing Top Fuel Chevrolet dragster is on permanent display at the Don Garlits Museum of Drag Racing.

In 1973, former "T.V. Tommy" Ivo mechanic John "Tarzan" Austin assumed the driving duties of South Florida sports fisherman Greg Schiegert's *Hot Tuna*, a Woody Gilmore-chassis rear-engine Top Fueler. For a rookie, Austin did a pretty respectable job, running all three championship circuits—AHRA, IHRA, and NHRA. Although Austin didn't score any major event wins, he nonetheless had fun taunting former boss Ivo, reminding him that it was "only a matter of time" before the two men would face each other on the racetrack. That fateful day finally arrived during Top Fuel eliminations at the 1974 NHRA Winternationals at Pomona, California. Unfortunately, it was an indecisive win for Austin, as Ivo fireballed his engine mid-track in his brand-new Ron Attebury car. The ensuing crash made all the newspapers and magazines. So, in a manner of speaking, even though Ivo lost the battle, he definitely won the war.

Edmonton, Alberta, Top Fuel driver Gary Beck burst onto the national event scene on August 27, 1972, when he made his Top Fuel driving debut at the NHRA Winston Championship Series event in Seattle. He piloted the Lawrence, Beck & Peets Reliable Engines AA/FD, carding a 6.30-220.00 the first time out. At Indy that year, the rapidly improving Beck triumphed over a stellar Top Fuel field that included the likes of Bob Fritchey, Randy Allison, the late Chuck Kurzawa, Herm Petersen, and Jerry "King" Ruth in the final to become the NHRA's very first Top Fuel champion from Canada.

The following year, Beck got off to a slow start but began building momentum by first winning the *Popular Hot Rodding* Magazine Championships over Pat Dakin. Then, Beck defended his title at Indy by beating Kuhl & Olson in the final. More important, the Canadian also set Low E.T. of the Meet with a blistering 5.96-240.44 in the semifinal round against Dennis Baca.

The 1974 season saw Beck & Peets sign a fairly lucrative sponsorship deal with the Canadian cigarette manufacturer Export A, which afforded them the additional finances and exposure needed by an emerging Top Fuel team. That year it became more of a question of what *didn't* Beck win, as the Canadian captured, among other things, the Top Fuel title at the NHRA Winternationals, the NHRA Springnationals, and a win at the Le Grandnational-Molson event at Sanair, Quebec. Beck finished the year as NHRA's Top Fuel World Champion. In the process he also won the AHRA World Finals at Spokane, Washington, which effectively gave him two crowns to wear.

The team of Beck & Peets continued racing well into the late 1970s, with event wins that included the 1976 PDA Meet at OCIR. However, sponsor changes and sporadic performances did not compare to the incredible consistency posted during the team's formative years. By the end of the decade Beck was semi-retired, living in Southern California, and working in the construction industry. However, history can and does repeat itself. In 1980, potato farmer Larry Minor coaxed Beck out of retirement, and the end result was the Beck & Minor juggernaut that ruled NHRA Top Fuel Eliminator action throughout the early 1980s.

Obviously, track conditions were right at the Mattel Hot Wheels Supernationals on November 16–17, 1972, when Mike "Hawaiian" Snively piloted "Diamond Jim" Annin's Top Fuel dragster to an unbelievable 5.97-235.60, to become the first driver in the 5s at an NHRA national event. Then, as if almost on a dare, veteran Top Fuel handler Don Moody (Walton, Cerny & Moody) reset the bar, recording an even quicker 5.91-231.95, besting Vic Brown in the Creitz & Donovan car on the final! Incredible performances like this were commonplace with WC&M, who set a total of eight E.T. records (from 6.37 to 5.91-seconds) in two-and-a-half years, as well as four MPH records ranging from a 321.36 top-end charge at Bakersfield on March 8, 1970, to a 233.76 on August 21, 1971, at Lions Associated Drag Strip. Other wins included the 1972 PRA Challenge at Tulsa, Oklahoma, where the team defeated Dennis Baca in the final, as well as setting Top Speed of the Meet at 229.00. WC&M also won Top Fuel at the 1973 Irwindale Grand Prix. Notice that Moody is wearing an open-face helmet and leather facemask instead of the traditional full-face helmet. Looks kind of sinister, doesn't he?

In 1972, the Division 7 Top Fuel team of Kuhl & Olson signed a deal with Revell, Inc. and they became known as "Da Revell Fast Guys." K&O had some rather interesting things happen to this car, like blowing off all the body panels at a Winston World Championship Series race in Washington State and sawing an engine in half at OCIR. However, during less stressful moments, the team managed to run a 5.94 on March 10, 1974, winning the Bakersfield March Meet. K&O were also runners-up to Marvin "Who" Graham at the 1975 OCIR PDA Championships, and finished in the runner-up spot to Gary Beck at the 1974 NHRA Springnationals.

"Kansas John" Wiebe and his Donovan-engine Don Long Top Fuel car squared off against "Big Daddy" Don Garlits and *Swamp Rat XIX* at the 1974 NHRA Gatornationals in Gainesville, Florida. *SR XIX* carried Garlits to his first 5-second clocking, running a 5.95 on July 7, 1973, at Portland and admitting Garlits into the exclusive Cragar Five Second Club. Conversely, Wiebe went on to become the 1975 and 1976 AHRA Top Fuel champion.

This is "Big Daddy" Don Garlits' *SR XXII* at the 1975 NHRA Gatornationals in Gainesville, Florida. On October 11, 1975, Garlits made drag racing history driving *Swamp Rat XXII* at the NHRA Winston Finals held at Ontario Motor Speedway, recording a top-end charge of 250.69 at 5.63-seconds. Two years later, this number was unofficially broken by Shirley Muldowney, first at the PRA Race held at Tucson Dragway in January 1977 (252.80) and in May at OCIR, where she ran a 253.52. However, Garlits' clocking "officially" remained in the NHRA Record Books for seven years, until Candies & Hughes driver Mark Oswald eclipsed those long-standing numbers at both Pomona, California, (5.618-seconds) and at Brainerd, Minnesota, (256.41). This is also the same car that Garlits won the first-ever NHRA Winston Top Fuel title with. To this day, Garlits regards his 250.69 top-end charge at Ontario as being, "the most famous run of my career!"

In the early 1970s, I was privileged to become friends with Shirley Muldowney through my long association with Amalie Refining Company, which was one of Muldowney's earliest sponsors. After nearly half a decade getting burned driving fuel Funny Cars, Top Fuel Eliminator was quite literally a breath of fresh air for the Mt. Clemens, Michigan-based Muldowney. Her Top Fuel public debut occurred at the 1975 NHRA Winternationals, where things went well enough, despite the fact that she neither won nor stayed around long in eliminations. Muldowney was nonetheless big news and the star of the show!

Her performances would improve over the summer so much that come NHRA Springnationals time Muldowney was running in the 230-mph zone with E.T.s in the 6.30s. She qualified well at Columbus and made her way through a tough field to face Marvin "Who" Graham in the final. However, Graham triumphed with 6.19-219.51 over Muldowney's 6.36-236.76.

At Indy 1975, Muldowney again qualified well in the field and eventually found herself in the finals going up against none other than "Big Daddy" Don Garlits. She lost to the man she affectionately refers to as "Donald," with a tire-spinning 6.44-191.08 to Garlits' winning 5.93-242.58.

With a full year's experience under her belt, Muldowney returned with a vengeance, celebrating our nation's bicentennial year with a few victory celebrations of her own. At the NHRA Springnationals she triumphed over Bob Edwards to win her first ever "Wally" NHRA event trophy. After Columbus, she ventured up to Martin, Michigan, where she recorded the track's first ever 5-second time at 5.98-seconds. Muldowney closed out the season by winning Top Fuel at the NHRA Winston Finals soundly, defeating Jerry "King" Ruth with a 5.94-248.61 to Ruth's 6.24-184.04!

Muldowney's meteoric rise to Top Fuel superstardom kicked into high gear in 1977. She began by setting Top Speed of the Meet at the PRA Winternationals race in Tucson, Arizona, in January 1977, unofficially eclipsing Garlits' two-year-old record, clocking a 252.80. She also set Top Speed of the Meet at the NHRA Winternationals at 248.61. In May, Muldowney again broke her personal MPH record, posting a 253.52 top-end charge at the PDA race at OCIR. She went on to win the NHRA Springnationals over Englishman Clive Skilton. After winning the NHRA Summernationals at Englishtown, New Jersey, and the NHRA Le Grandnational-Molson race at Sanair, Canada, she handily won the NHRA Winston Top Fuel Championship, a feat she repeated in both 1980 and 1983. Shirley also won the PDA Championship Race on July 17 in Seattle, defeating R. Gaines Markley in the final. That year, Muldowney was voted *Car Craft* Magazine's "Person of the Year" and was inducted as a member of *Car Craft*'s All-Star Drag Racing Team.

Muldowney's career flourished into the early 1980s until her much-publicized accident at Sanair in 1984. She won Pomona in 1978, and again in 1983. She won Indy in 1982, and to this day holds the distinction of being the U.S. Nationals' only female Top Fuel title-holder. She also won the AHRA Top Fuel title in 1983.

The motion picture *Heart Like a Wheel*, starring Bonnie Bedelia and Beau Bridges, made Muldowney's name a household word with mainstream America. Suffice it to say that throughout the 1970s and 1980s, Muldowney was revered as one of America's most respected and cherished female athletes.

In the summer of 1975, New York National Speedway in Center Moriches, Long Island, New York, was the site of the Professional Racers Association (PRA) National Challenge. This was quite an excursion for many of the western region Top Fuel racers who attended the event, like Denver's Junior Kaiser and Southern Californians Cyr & Schofield, Larry Dixon Sr. (*Howard's Cams Rat*), and Bruce Walker, who drove Childs & Albert's *Addict*. After appearing at a press preview party on Coney Island's famed boardwalk, where "Broadway Freddie" de Name made an unscheduled burnout with his Camaro Funny Car, the race itself—which was plagued with malfunctioning clocks and total chaos—seemed almost anticlimactic. On the final, "Kansas John" Wiebe's clock malfunctioned, but he crossed the finish line first, beating Bruce Walker for the money. This late afternoon shot was taken of Junior Kaiser in the Kaiser Bros. entry charging hard off New York National's starting line. New York National Speedway closed in the 1980s, and now the strip is the main entry road to, of all things, a trailer park!

BELOW: Here we see Walt "Wally the Gator" Rhoades ready to blast off into the Southern California twilight during OCIR's 7th Annual PDA Championships in the summer of 1974. Rhoades was one of NHRA Division 7's most respected Top Gas drivers in the late 1960s and early 1970s, having piloted such cars as the twin-engine *Freight Train* (Walt won the 1972 NHRA Gatornationals with John Peters Chrysler power) and the Ken's Automotive *Odd Couple* Chrysler/Chevrolet twin-engine gas dragster. In 1977, Rhoades was runner-up to Keeling & Clayton driver Rick Ramsey at the very last PDA Championship event held at OCIR, prior to him retiring from driving fuel cars.

Here's a shot of Warren, Coburn & Miller doing what they do best: running incredible top-end speeds. The debut of the Ridge Route Terrors' first of two rear-engine Top Fuel dragsters was in 1973. There's so much to cover here . . . How about a 5.97 clocking on October 13, 1973, at Fremont? Or how about winning the 1973 PDA Championships at OCIR where they ran a 6.41-227.84 to beat none other than "Big Daddy" Don Garlits? Or perhaps setting both Top Speed (248.61) and Low E.T. of the Meet (5.88-seconds) at the 1974 NHRA World Finals? Then, too, it's hard to overlook a total of four NHRA/NHRA-Winston Division 7 Top Fuel Championships, which were equally divided between their 392-powered rear-engine digger and the team's all-new late-model Hemi car. WC&M also bear the distinction of having won the Bakersfield March Meet in 1975–77, while consistently setting either (or both) Top Speed and Low E.T. of the Meet! The team also won the Irwindale Grand Prix in 1974, setting both Top Speed of the Meet (241.93) and Low E.T. (5.99), along with winning a veritable ton of other local Top Fuel shows up and down the West Coast. This particular photo of James Warren in the lights at OCIR with the laundry just starting to come out is one of my (previously unpublished) favorites.

In the mid 1970s, NHRA Division 7 hopefuls Brissette, Noice & Crader campaigned this Donovan-powered Woody Gilmore AA/FD locally with reasonable success, running a best of 6.00 at 238.00. But every once in awhile, Brissette, Noice & Crader ventured outside California to test the waters. Such was the case at the 1972 NHRA U.S. Nationals at Indy, where I clicked this wide-angle photo of Bob Noice jumping on the "loud pedal." Incidentally, in later days Noice won Top Fuel (Brissette, Noice & Drake) at the 1979 NHRA Winternationals.

This classic rear-engine confrontation happened during eliminations at the 1974 NHRA U.S. Nationals between Sarge Arciero driving the Asher, Fluerer & Arciero *Jade Grenade*, and Terry Capp in the Capp & Van Duesen *Wheeler Dealer*. Note that both of these machines are equipped with front wheel fairings, another Nye Frank invention that was tried briefly during the formative years of rear-engine Top Fuel. If memory serves me correctly, Capp won this match. Earlier that summer, Capp & Van Duesen won Top Fuel at the one and only AHRA Challenge, defeating "Kansas John" Wiebe in the final and setting Top Speed (234.37) and Low E.T. of the Meet (6.20-seconds). Some years later (1980) the team would win the biggest race of them all, beating Jeb Allen at Indy in the final. Throughout the years there has been some confusion concerning the origins of the name *Wheeler Dealer*. In the mid 1960s NHRA Division 1 Top Fuel racer Bruce Wheeler (and later Tom Chastang) raced a pair of Top Fuel cars on the eastern seaboard named the *Wheeler Dealer*. Conversely, the Capp & Van Duesen *Wheeler Dealer* (which hailed from Edmonton, Alberta) got its name from Capp's sponsor, Edmonton's Wheeler Dealer Performance Center. That ought to clear up some of the confusion!

"Napa Frank" Bradley, a professional plumber by trade, was one of those Top Fuel racers who didn't win a lot of races, but he was always there. Credits include a Top Fuel win at the 1991 NHRA Winternationals over Don "Snake" Prudhomme (at 4.998-seconds in Pomona, California, on October 25, 1989) and a #10 spot on the exclusive Cragar Five Second Club roster. Bradley was also runner-up in Top Fuel to "Hollywood Kelly" Brown at the 1978 NHRA Springnationals and to Shirley Muldowney at the 1980 NHRA-Winston Finals. Prior to Bradley's retirement, he also claimed the dubious distinction of becoming the AHRA's final E.T. and MPH record holder, at 5.53-225.31.

This car, which also appears on the cover of this book, is from the Brooklyn, Michigan-based Fighting Irish Top Fuel team of Beebe & Murphy, which was an extension of the original Southern California-based Beebe Bros., Vinson & Sixt Top Fuel team from the early 1960s. Confused? I'm happy to explain.

In the early 1960s, Dave and Tim "Chops" Beebe raced a Bantam-bodied AA/FA out on the West Coast with reasonable success. In 1965, they went Top Fuel racing, forming the team of Beebe Bros., Vinson & Sixt. When Dave left a year later, John "Zookeeper" Mulligan jumped into the driver's seat, and the team became known as the Fighting Irish. From 1967 to 1969, Beebe & Mulligan were one of the most feared Top Fuel teams in all the land. With the untimely passing of Mulligan in October 1969, Tim took a little time off prior to teaming up with brother Dave on a '70 Dodge Challenger Funny Car that they had leased from Salt Lake City's Ferguson and Hoffines. It, too, was called the *Fighting Irish*.

Then in 1971, Dave left—again—and Tim built a new *Fighting Irish* mini-Camaro with driver Dick Rosberg installed behind the wheel. Beebe & Rosberg successfully toured both the Camaro and later the *Fighting Irish* Plymouth Satellite AA/FC. Then Tim and transplanted Northern California building contractor/fuel Funny Car racer Jim "Holy Smokes" Murphy joined forces to campaign the Beebe & Murphy Fighting Irish rear-engine AA/FDs (there were two), which primarily competed on the UDRA Midwest circuit. In fact, Beebe & Murphy were the 1973 circuit champs. Unfortunately, the team never really knocked down any major event wins, but man, could old Murph do some killer burnouts, as witnessed by this shot taken at Gainesville 1974!

It's the battle of the nitro-burning Chevrolets! This photo was taken at one of the last NHRA Winston Finals events held at OCIR around 1982. Racing in the far lane is the world's first 5-second Chevrolet, and the only Chevrolet ever to nail down a spot in the exclusive Cragar Five Second Club at 5.97-seconds on November 16, 1973, by the Dixon, Dunne & Anthony *Howard's Cams Rat*, driven by Larry Dixon Sr. In the tower lane is the team of Oswald & Williams, who routinely ran low 6s with their car. To my knowledge, the Top Fuel team of Lidtke-Zeller, with Stan Shiroma driving, is the only other officially recognized 5-second Chevrolet in the sport, clocking 5.86-seconds in January 1976 at the Irwindale Grand Prix.

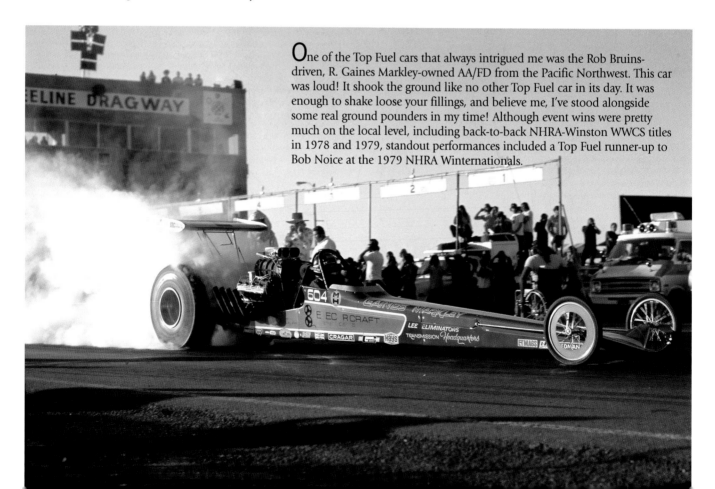

One of the Top Fuel cars that always intrigued me was the Rob Bruins-driven, R. Gaines Markley-owned AA/FD from the Pacific Northwest. This car was loud! It shook the ground like no other Top Fuel car in its day. It was enough to shake loose your fillings, and believe me, I've stood alongside some real ground pounders in my time! Although event wins were pretty much on the local level, including back-to-back NHRA-Winston WWCS titles in 1978 and 1979, standout performances included a Top Fuel runner-up to Bob Noice at the 1979 NHRA Winternationals.

Surprisingly, mid 1960s rear-engine Top Gas dragster proponent Tony "Loner" Nancy (the *Wedge* and *Wedge II* AA/GDs) was a late entry in the rear-engine Top Fuel wars with his incredibly beautiful Kent Fuller-chassis *Revell-liner*, circa 1974. However, Nancy made up for lost time with runner-up performances at both the 1974 and 1976 March Meets at Bakersfield. Obviously, Nancy's *Revell-liner* also ran hard enough to qualify at Indy 1976, where we see him in the top photo racing fellow NHRA Division 7 racer Don Moody. Nancy's extremely lucrative automotive upholstery restoration business with a list of high-profile clients, combined with his ever-growing involvement as a transportation consultant to the motion picture industry, led Nancy to retire in the late 1970s. Just prior to his passing, though, Nancy made one last appearance at the 2004 California Hot Rod Reunion's highly touted Cacklefest sitting behind the wheel of his last front-engine car, the famed *Superior Sizzler* AA/FD that won the 1970 Bakersfield March Meet.

Historical records indicate that Jack Martin was the first rear-engine Top Fuel driver to experience what they now call a "blow over" while competing in a brand new (unpainted) rear-engine dragster at the AHRA Grand American Championship at Lions Associated Drag Strip in January 1971. However, "Big Daddy" Don Garlits' Englishtown blow over and Eddie "The Thrill" Hill's Pomona blow over are clearly the most publicized.

The fact of the matter is that Top Fuel drivers have been getting it up since the very beginning. I call this my "wheelie page," because I happen to have caught a number of top-flight (excuse the pun) Top Fuel pilots during takeoff. Fortunately, none of these guys took it to the extremes, although you sure couldn't tell it by looking at some of these pictures. They are Pat Dakin in the G.L. Rupp car racing Charlie Moulder in the *Hoppin' Gator* at IHRA Rockingham in 1974 (above); NHRA Winternationals 1981 winner Jeb Allen grabbing air at Pomona that same year (below); Dick LaHaie reaching for Pomona skies in 1984 (opposite top); Top Fuel pilot "Flying Fred" Farndon at the NHRA Winternationals, circa 1985 (sequence, opposite); and last is Denver Top Fuel driver Junior Kaiser one-wheeling it at the 1986 edition of the NHRA U.S. Nationals at Indianapolis Raceway Park.

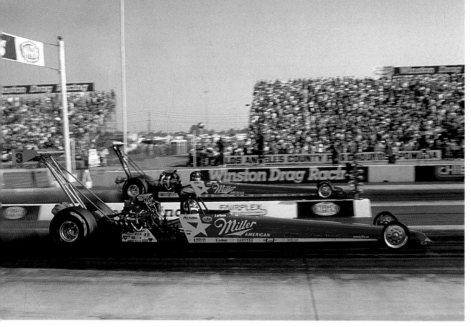

Although I didn't attend that many NHRA Championship Drag Races toward the end of the 1980s, I did enjoy a few incredible moments. One of them was watching multiple NHRA Top Fuel Champ Gary Beck square off against boss Larry Minor in an all-Miller American matchup at Pomona 1984. As you can see, the boss was out on the champ, and it stayed that way. Minor ran a best of 5.40 at Pomona, only to lose to eventual winner Joe Amato.

In the five years that Beck & Minor raced together, they collectively produced 30 low E.T. clockings at NHRA and IHRA national events and/or points meets, ranging between a 5.71 for Beck on March 16, 1980, at Gainesville and a 5.32 for Minor on October 24, 1980, at Pomona. During Beck's 1983 NHRA-Winston Championship season, he also ran an unprecedented 17 out of 18 low E.T.s in Minor's dragster, according to Chris Martin's *The Top Fuel Handbook*.

Major event wins included a win at the 1983 IHRA Springnationals against Richard Tharp; winner of the 1988 NHRA Winternationals, with Dick LaHaie driving; and winner of the 1981 NHRA Springnationals (Beck) over Jim and Allison Lee and the 1984 NHRA Springnationals over Joe Amato. Beck also won Indy in 1983 against Amato, the 1981 NHRA-Winston Finals at OCIR against Ray Fisher, and finished in the runner-up spot to Jim Barnard at the 1982 NHRA Winston Finals.

Title wins at the "Big Shows" also included winning the 1982 *Popular Hot Rodding* Championships against Jody Smart (Beck also set Top Speed and Low E.T. at 250.00-5.65-seconds), as well as a clean sweep of the 1984 March Meet, where Beck ran a 5.49-253.52 to defeat Minor at 5.67-256.41. Beck set Top Speed at 262.39 and Low E.T. with a 5.41, and retained his title the following year by defeating Ed Harmon.

Pennsylvanian Joe Amato first started racing a BB/FC in NHRA competition in the early 1970s. However, by 1984 Amato had worked his way through the ranks and went Top Fuel racing. Amato was what you call a mile-an-hour guy, setting Top Speed at NHRA events 25 times from 1984 to 1995. However, his greatest feat was breaking the 260-mph barrier not once but twice on the same day, at Gainesville 1984 at 260.11 and 262.30. This car flat thundered! Amato went on to win the NHRA-Winston Top Fuel Championship a total of five times: 1984, 1988, and 1990–'92.

This isn't the comeback photo of the year; it's the comeback photo of the decade! After Shirley Muldowney's near-fatal top-end crash at the 1984 Le Grandnational-Molson race at Sanair, Quebec, Canada, speculation ran high that she would never return. Yeah, right! Those skeptics just didn't know Muldowney like we know her. In January 1986, she was back behind the wheel of a brand new Top Fuel car with sponsorship from PAW's Keith Harvey. This classic match-up between "Big Daddy" Don Garlits and Muldowney at the 1986 NHRA Winternationals brought everyone to their feet. And while Garlits took the match, everybody in the house knew that Muldowney was back!

In 1986, Gary Ormsby entered this carbon fiber body, Castrol-sponsored Top Fuel streamliner in NHRA Winternationals competition. Unfortunately, a spark plug wire shorted out against the carbon fiber bodywork, and "kaboom!" Ultimately, the streamliner idea was scrapped, and Ormsby returned to the more conventional body design and ran it the rest of the season.

In 1989, Gary Ormsby was back and better than ever, winning Top Fuel Eliminator at Pomona, Houston, Montreal, Dallas, and finally, the NHRA Winston Finals back at Pomona to annex his first and only NHRA-Winston Top World Championship. Unfortunately, Ormsby lost the ultimate race against cancer on August 28, 1991. His headstone, which is located in the city of his birth in Sand Springs, Oklahoma, proudly declares, "Gary Lewis Ormsby, 1989 NHRA-Winston World Champion!" Ormsby was also a member of the super-exclusive Cragar Four Second Club, clocking a 4.991 at Columbus, Ohio, on June 10, 1989.

One of drag racing's most promising superstars was 28-year-old Darrell Gwynn, former NHRA Winston-Top Alcohol Dragster champ and up-and-coming Top Fuel driver. Unfortunately, a crippling top-end crash at Santa Pod Raceway while touring England on Easter Sunday 1990 nearly cost Gwynn his life, leaving him a quadriplegic. Most guys in his position would have just given up, but not Gwynn! Through the help and support of both his immediate and extended families, he continues to race, albeit through the eyes, hands, and minds of drivers like Frank Hawley and Mike Dunn. At the 1990 NHRA Springnationals, Darrell Gwynn Racing unveiled the Coors Extra Gold Top Fuel dragster driven by Hawley, which handily won the event—career win 29 for Gwynn and his family. Today, Gwynn continues to compete in the NHRA-POWERade Top Fuel Championship. After all, you just can't keep a good man down!

Chapter 3

FUNNIES

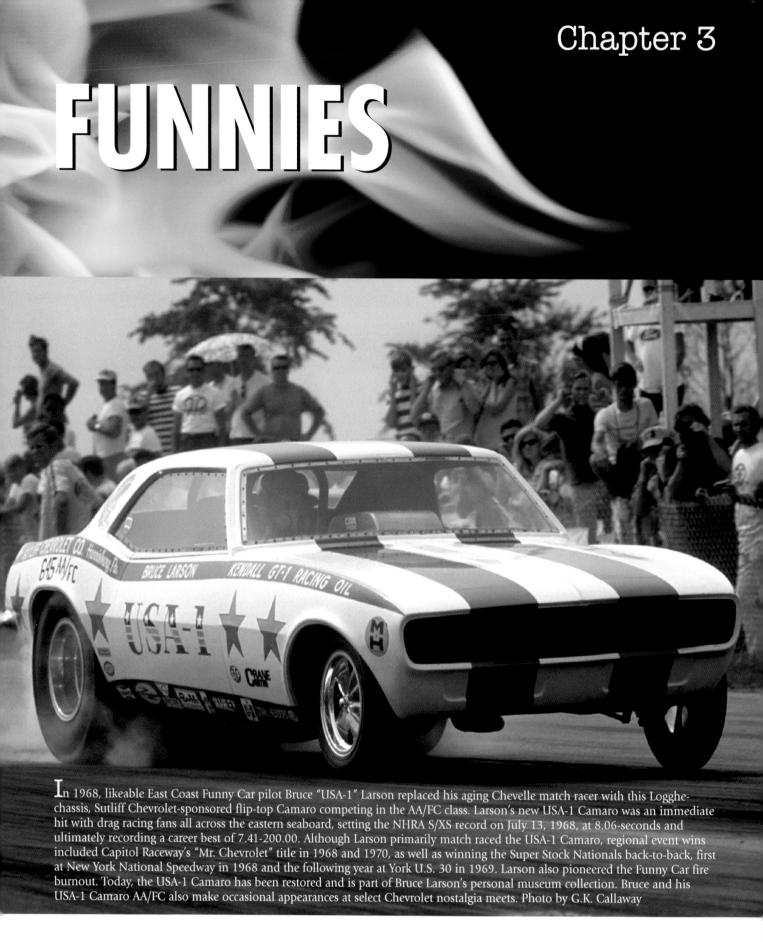

In 1968, likeable East Coast Funny Car pilot Bruce "USA-1" Larson replaced his aging Chevelle match racer with this Logghe-chassis, Sutliff Chevrolet-sponsored flip-top Camaro competing in the AA/FC class. Larson's new USA-1 Camaro was an immediate hit with drag racing fans all across the eastern seaboard, setting the NHRA S/XS record on July 13, 1968, at 8.06-seconds and ultimately recording a career best of 7.41-200.00. Although Larson primarily match raced the USA-1 Camaro, regional event wins included Capitol Raceway's "Mr. Chevrolet" title in 1968 and 1970, as well as winning the Super Stock Nationals back-to-back, first at New York National Speedway in 1968 and the following year at York U.S. 30 in 1969. Larson also pioneered the Funny Car fire burnout. Today, the USA-1 Camaro has been restored and is part of Bruce Larson's personal museum collection. Bruce and his USA-1 Camaro AA/FC also make occasional appearances at select Chevrolet nostalgia meets. Photo by G.K. Callaway

W hat better place to begin this chapter than on the starting line at Lions Associated Drag Strip, circa 1965, where we find the late, great Dick Harrell and his Z11 engine *Retribution II* 1965 Chevy II stocker grabbing air during a match race against the Tom "Mongoose" McEwen-driven *Hemi 'Cuda*. In January 1965, Harrell set the A/FX record at the AHRA Winternationals with this car with a 10.24 at 127.80. However, by midyear, Harrell's Chevy II had been converted into a full-on match racer, the effects of which are clearly illustrated by this bumper-dragging wheel stand. Prior to being replaced by an even more potent Bill Thomas Race Cars-built 1966 match-race Nova, Harrell's *Retribution II* ran a career best of around 10 seconds flat! Photos by G.K. Callaway

T aking a cue from Jack Chrisman's phenomenally successful supercharged 1964 Mercury Comet Cyclone, Chrisman's Comet Top Fuel campaigner Lou Baney, who worked for and owned an interest in the Dowey, California-based Yeakel Plymouth franchise, got together in early 1965 with the L.A. Plymouth Dealer's Association and proposed an exciting new Mopar match race stocker that had all the outer appearances of a modern day muscle car yet performed like a Top Fuel dragster. The end result was the Ron Scrima/Pat Foster/B&M Automotive-built *Hemi 'Cuda*, the world's first rear-engine Funny Car.

Obviously, some very creative engineering was required in order to cram a blown, fuel-burning Dave Zeuschel-assembled 426 Plymouth Hemi engine into the back seat of a 1965 Plymouth Barracuda. A custom removable rear subframe needed to be built, and the aforementioned blown Hemi was hooked up to a B&M Tork Master V-Drive setup. Initial testing with Yeakel Plymouth Top Fuel dragster driver Tom "Mongoose" McEwen installed behind the wheel produced 160-mph terminal speeds, a performance promising enough to enter the car in the 1965 NHRA Winternationals where it competed in the CC/FD class. Ultimately, McEwen ran a best of 9.14-178.92 with the *Hemi 'Cuda*. Unfortunately, the *'Cuda* got airborne in the lights at Lions Associated Drag Strip in July 1965, and the car was a total write-off. Then *Hemi 'Cuda II* was built, but McEwen decided to return to his first love, Top Fuel dragsters. The L.A. Plymouth Dealer's Association then enlisted Fred Goeske to campaign the *Hemi 'Cuda II* in earnest. Ultimately, Goeske and the *Hemi 'Cuda II* ran in the mid 8s at 185 mph prior to the car's retirement in 1968. Photo by G.K. Callaway

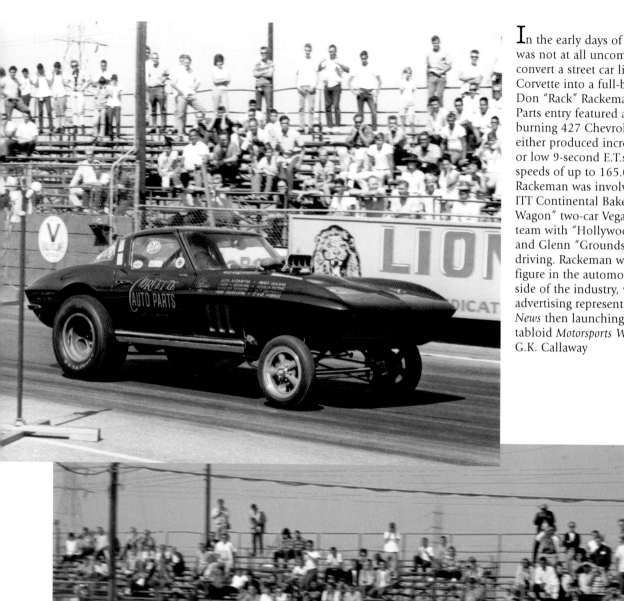

In the early days of Funny Cars, it was not at all uncommon for guys to convert a street car like this 1965 Corvette into a full-blown race car. Don "Rack" Rackeman's Corvette Auto Parts entry featured a blown, fuel-burning 427 Chevrolet big-block that either produced incredible wheelies, or low 9-second E.T.s and terminal speeds of up to 165.00. In later years, Rackeman was involved in the original ITT Continental Bakeries "Wonder Wagon" two-car Vega panel Funny Car team with "Hollywood Kelly" Brown and Glenn "Groundshakers" Way driving. Rackeman was also a key figure in the automotive publishing side of the industry, working as the advertising representative for *Drag News* then launching his own racing tabloid *Motorsports Weekly*. Photo by G.K. Callaway

The early days of Funny Car racing were indeed an era of experimentation, and there were often crossovers within the classes. One such example was the Southern California team of (Ralph) Snodgrass & (Pat) Mahnken, who originally campaigned this chassis with a Fiat Topolino body in the AA/FA class, powered by a blown, fuel-burning 406-427 "Wedge Head" Ford FE engine. Then in early 1966, Snodgrass & Mahnken converted the fuel-altered over to a Funny Car, complete with a two-piece Mustang fiberglass body. Appropriately named *Psycho*, the short wheelbase fuel burner definitely lived up to its name. The car was often entered in local shows, where it never failed to entertain the fans. Photo by G.K. Callaway

In late 1965, the team of Roger Wolford and Ed Lenarth obtained a fiberglass Jeep body that had been previously used in a Jeep television commercial through Placentia, California, off-road impresario Brian Chuchua. The two proceeded to go out and build drag racing's first Jeep Funny Car! The Dick Fletcher-chassis, Chrysler-powered *Secret Weapon*, sponsored by Chuchua's Four Wheel Drive Center, won the blown class (at 8.70-seconds) at the *Drag Strip* Magazine "East versus West" Funny Car Championships, held at Lions Associated Drag Strip in the fall of 1966. Unfortunately, engine fires constantly plagued the team, forcing them to rebuild the Jeep a number of times. As the late 1960s unfolded, the *Secret Weapon* evolved into a Jeepster Funny Car named the *Holy Toledo*, which made the rounds for a couple more years, running a best of 7.52-173.74. After disappearing from the quarter-mile arena, rumor had it that *Holy Toledo* had been converted into a sand racer prior to its restoration back to an AA/FC around 2002. Today, *Holy Toledo* can be found on display at drag racing nostalgia events like the Wally Parks-NHRA California Hot Rod Reunion, held the first weekend in October in Bakersfield, California. Photos by G.K. Callaway & Bob McClurg

In 1966, former AA/Modified Sports Car driver and 1965 NHRA Springnationals winner Bruce "USA-1" Larson parked his *Dragonsnake* 289 Shelby Cobra to race this all-fiberglass (a first for its time) 1966-67 Chevelle match racer, *USA-1*. The Chevelle would also be the first of a long line of Sutliff Chevrolet-sponsored (Harrisburg, Pennsylvania) USA-1 Chevrolets driven by the yet uncrowned 1989 NHRA-Winston Funny Car World Champion. Powered by a 427 fuel-injected big-block Semi-Hemi, Larson's *USA-1* Chevelle set the NHRA B/XS record at 8.85-159.00 on May 28, 1967. The Chevelle was equally as notorious on the match race circuit. Here we see Larson racing Ed Carter's *Chevy II Heavy* (the former Steve Bovan car) in the 2,600-pound class finale at the 1967 U.S. Fuel & Gas Championships in Bakersfield, California, on February 17–19, where *USA-1* ran mid 8s at 159 mph. Larson's *USA-1* Chevelle has since been restored, and is on permanent display at the Don Garlits Museum of Drag Racing.

At Lions Associated Drag Strip, I caught Clyde Morgan and the *Vicious 'Vette* (Morgan & Wilson) in action against Comet team driver Pete "Gate Job" Gates. Although Morgan is out on the 1966 Super Stock Nationals winner, Gates' 427 SOHC powered Mercury Comet made up the difference on the big end. In those early days, I often hitched a ride with the *Vicious 'Vette* team to local races, and I owe a tremendous debt of gratitude to Morgan (who today races offshore powerboats) and car owner Charlie Wilson, who lost his life driving a Funny Car in the early 1970s. The *Vicious 'Vette* was capable of running 9.30s at over 155 mph, which was pretty darned good for a car that weighed around 3,000 pounds!

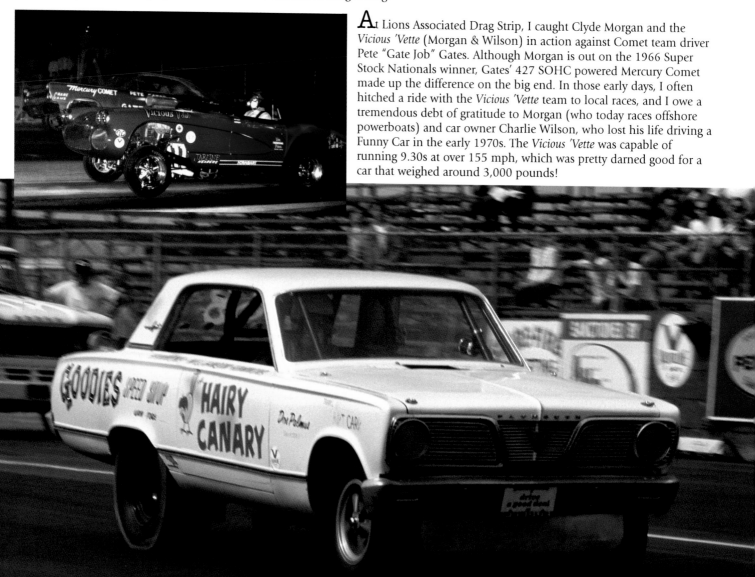

The *Hairy Canary* Plymouth Valiant of Hammons, Williamson & Hammons made its grand debut in 1967 as part of Rich Guess' four-car Goodies Speed Shop Racing Team, which also included Lew Arrington's *Brutus* GTO, "Jungle Jim" Liberman's Chevy Nova, and Rich Abate's *Sampson* Dodge Dart.

"They didn't call it the *Hairy Canary* for nothing," commented veteran drag racing photojournalist Steve Reyes. "The car was equipped with an offset steering shaft that caused some rather unpredictable handling problems. In fact, I remember one time when Don Williamson drove the car at Carlsbad Raceway (Rich Hammons usually drove), and he stood it straight up on the back bumper in the lights!"

When the *Hairy Canary* did go straight, the yellow-hued 1966 Plymouth Valiant usually ran low 9s, recording terminal speeds in the 170s. Recent reports are that the *Hairy Canary* is being replicated for display at nostalgia drag races. Hmm, I wonder if the new car will be built with that same weird offset steering setup? Photo by G.K. Callaway

This is a scene from the 1966 *Hot Rod* Magazine Drags where Jim Whetton, driving the ex-"Dandy Dick" Landy 1965 altered-wheelbase *Studio Dodge*, is going up against Tommy Grove's "Ford Charger" long-wheelbase Holman & Moody Mustang for the Experimental Stock title. Grove had just returned home from a win over Maynard Rupp at the NHRA Springnationals at Bristol, Tennessee, and definitely was on a hot streak. Photo by G.K. Callaway

In 1967, Venolia Pistons Company President Joe Pisano and his brother Frankie fielded this Doug Kruse-built half-steel, half-fiberglass blown '67 S/XS Camaro, which ran a best of 8.50-seconds at 170 mph. Ultimately, the car proved a tad too heavy for serious match race Funny Car competition, and it was replaced late in the year with Doug Thorley's Indianapolis-winning S/XS Corvair. The Pisano brothers' first Camaro Funny Car nonetheless earned them a spot that year on *Car Craft* Magazine's "10 Best Rods of 1967" list. Photo by G.K. Callaway

On January 24, 2006, we lost one of drag racing's greatest competitors, "Dyno Don" Nicholson. Nicholson's beginnings go all the way back to the California dry lakes era, when he used to race Chevrolets with his brother Harold. Don Nicholson also used to race his Wayne-headed '34 Chevrolet sedan out at the old El Toro Marine Blimp Base even before there was such a thing as the Santa Ana Drags. Of course, he became one of the West Coast's premiere stocker drivers, wheeling his '61 409-engine Chevrolet Bel Air to the Stock Eliminator title at the inaugural NHRA Winternationals in Pomona, California.

"That's still the most memorable race of my career," Nicholson said to me during an interview for *Mustang Illustrated*. "When we drove up the return road after winning the race, the fans stood up and cheered for us from one end of the bleachers to the other!"

Where did the "Dyno Don" nickname come from? "That came from my early days working in the dynamometer room at C.S. Mead Chevrolet in Pasadena, California," Nicholson said. "Once the promoters got wind of it, it just sort of stuck."

Nicholson's prowess as a match racer was renown. In 1961, he became one of the sport's first touring professionals, but not with a Top Fuel dragster, a gasser, or some other form of exotic race car. Rather, it was with a lowly stocker!

"In 1961, I read an ad in *Drag News* that stated a promoter down south was running a Super Stock meet with a thousand dollars to win," Nicholson said. "We (he and his wife Patty) soon realized that we could run a couple of meets within a week or so and pick up a thousand dollars here, five hundred dollars there, or two or three hundred dollars here. Heck, out on the West Coast we were running for $25 savings bonds, so about $18.50 was about all you could really win. I called a couple of these guys up and said that I would be willing to attend if they would pay me a little tow money, and they said yes!"

In no time at all, Nicholson had his '61 Bel Air hooked up to the back bumper of mechanic Earl Wade's '57 Chevy and they were on their way. Nicholson won that first event handily and never looked back.

Somewhere around 1963, Nicholson purchased a home in Atlanta and went to work in the dyno room at Nalle Chevrolet. One day, NASCAR racer Troy Ruttman walked through the door with a couple of Lincoln-Mercury executives in tow. "We all got to talking, and they invited us up to Detroit. Lincoln-Mercury was willing to provide us with the cars, and all the parts. In the end, it proved to be a winning association."

Nicholson's first Mercury was, of all things, a one-off 427 engine Mercury Comet station wagon known as the *Ugly Duckling*, which set Low E.T. for the A/FX class at the 1964 NHRA Winternationals in Pomona at 11.34-seconds. Nicholson was also runner-up to the late Ronnie Sox's 427 Comet Caliente in Factory Stock Eliminator with an 11.47 to Sox's slightly slower 11.49. Unfortunately, Chrysler lobbied to have the wagon outlawed shortly thereafter. Nicholson's next car was a more conventional 427-engine '64 Comet Caliente, which he used to set the NHRA A/FX MPH record with an 11.09 at Indy, and he finished the season at the top of the *Drag News* "Mr. Stock Eliminator" list.

The following season, Nicholson was one of the lucky drivers given a handful of Bill Stroppe-built 427 SOHC Mercury Comet Cyclones, which he started out running as a legal A/FX car, setting records and winning races like the 1965 NHRA Springnationals—running as quick as 10.56-131.96. But by the end of the season he had converted the Comet over to a full on fuel-injected altered-wheelbase match racer capable of running mid 9.30s at 150 mph. That is, whenever he could get the car to go straight.

"That was the scariest car I ever drove," Nicholson commented. "When we first got that car running, I was at Martin, Michigan. It was at night, and the lights weren't all that good, especially in the shutoff area. The car was squirrelly all the way down the track. When I got to the other end I said, 'Boy, Nicholson, you made it again!'"

The following season, Nicholson and Team Mercury revolutionized Funny Car racing with the introduction of the Logghe chassis flip-top Comet Cyclone Funny Cars. "It was just progress. We wanted to go faster, and this was the safest way to do it," he said.

Safe and fast! Nicholson's *Eliminator 1* was the class of the field. It was the first Funny Car in the 7s and sported an incredible 90 percent win/loss record. Among a seemingly endless list of accomplishments, *Drag Strip* Magazine readers voted *Eliminator 1* as the number-one injected Funny Car in the nation for 1967.

My favorite Nicholson car was his candy apple red '66 Logghe-chassis *Eliminator II*, which won eight straight races right out of the box! The early season addition of a supercharger only quickened the pace, running in the 7.90s at 181+ mph by season's end. The following season Nicholson again dominated with his *Eliminator* Cougar Funny Car. Unfortunately, engine fires and the loss of one of two Cougar Funny Cars from a towing accident took all the fun out of Funny Car racing for Nicholson. By the end of the 1968 racing season, he was out of the car for good.

In 1969, Nicholson, Ronnie Sox and Buddy Martin, "Dandy Dick" Landy, and Bill "Grumpy" Jenkins united to form the United States Drag Racing Team, which was the forerunner of AHRA/IHRA/NHRA Pro Stock. More on that in chapter five.

I first met Nicholson in 1965 at Bill Stroppe's Signal Hill, California, shop where the 427 SOHC A/FX Comets were being built. As I plied my trade and started showing up at various racetracks across the country where Nicholson was running, we developed a casual friendship that became stronger as the years rolled by.

Sitting in my trophy case at home is a pair of black and gold 427 SOHC Ford valve covers that Nicholson gave to me in 1979 when *Hot Rod* Magazine Tech Editor C.J. Baker and I visited Nicholson at his Atlanta shop. They reputedly are off Nicholson's *Eliminator II*, and today they are amongst some of my most prized collectibles.

In 1967, former "outlaw" AA/GS racer Steve Montrelli (Korney & Montrelli's *Goldfinger* Chrysler Anglia) went Funny Car racing with this Dick Fletcher-chassis, Chrysler-powered, Don Kirby-painted, Fiberglass Trends-bodied, Montrelli, Williams & Barrett *New Breed* Pontiac Firebird. Driven by partner Tom Barrett, the *New Breed* immediately showed promise, running an 8.48-174.00 right off the trailer. However, like a lot of Funny Car racers in those days, finances kept the team from ever taking it to the national event level. Of course, Montrelli went on to start up his own company, Steve Montrelli Racing Engines, which serviced the Top Fuel and Funny Car ranks for many years. Photo by G.K. Callaway

In 1967, former Arthur Murray Dance School instructor and 1964 NHRA Super Stock World Champion Gaspar "Gas" Ronda traded in his aging '66 Holman & Moody Mustang Funny Car for this Ronnie Scrima/Exhibition Engineering-constructed "clamshell" '67 Mustang flopper. The car is called a clamshell because both the front and rear fiberglass body sections of the car tilted up. Powered by a Cliff Brian-tuned, fuel-injected 427 SOHC Ford engine and carrying the logo of longtime sponsor Russ Davis Ford of Covina, California, Ronda's Mustang reeled off an incredible 7.67-seconds to nail down the NHRA E.T. world record for injected-fuel Funny Cars. Gaspar won a lot of races with this car. However, in 1968, Ronda was forced to convert the Mustang over to a blower, although he was less than pleased with the results.

"The 1968 car really wasn't (set up) right for a blown engine," Ronda told *Mustang Illustrated* Magazine in a spring 1988 issue. "We butchered the car so much just to make the engine fit. We goofed around and moved the engine back in the chassis. Finally, I realized toward the middle of the season that what I really needed was a new car setup to handle a (Ed Pink) blown engine. That's when I had Logghe Stamping Co. build me my last car, my Mach-1 Mustang that won the 1969 Manufacturer's Funny Car Team Championship at OCIR."

Unfortunately, a serious engine fire while competing at the 1970 AHRA Winternationals sidelined Ronda for good. After his retirement he opened up a bar in West Covina, appropriately named the Gas House, which he operated into the early 1990s. Today Ronda is retired and living the quiet life in Palm Springs with his wife, where he spends most of his time pursuing his other passion, playing golf. Photo by G.K. Callaway

Experimentation certainly was the name of the game in the early days of Funny Car racing. Take, for instance, Dick Jesse's *Mr. Unswitchable* '67 Pontiac GTO Funny Car. Is this baby severely chopped, or what? Suffice to say, Jesse's "Goat" really pushed the envelope. In fact, this is one of the early Funny Cars that ultimately forced the NHRA into instituting regulations regarding what could legally be done to a car body. Unfortunately, it was also the car in which Dick Jesse lost his life. Photo by G.K. Callaway

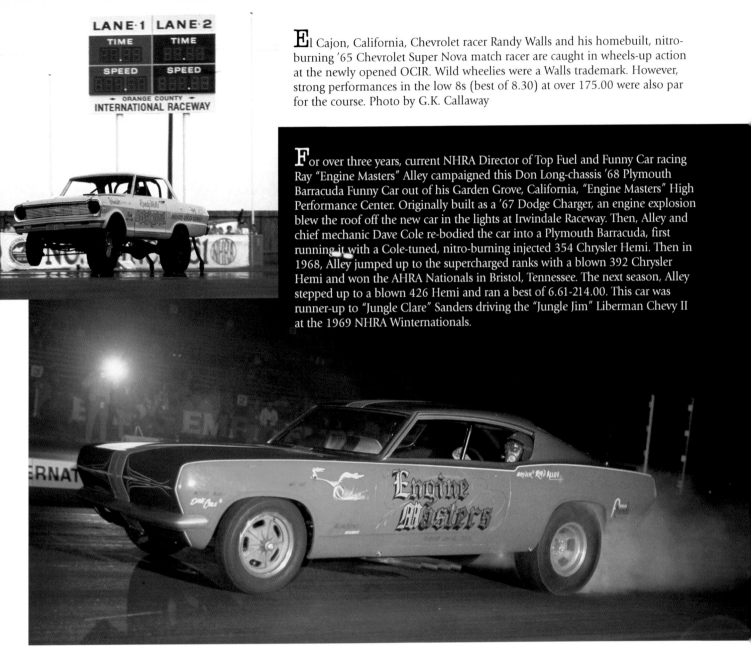

El Cajon, California, Chevrolet racer Randy Walls and his homebuilt, nitro-burning '65 Chevrolet Super Nova match racer are caught in wheels-up action at the newly opened OCIR. Wild wheelies were a Walls trademark. However, strong performances in the low 8s (best of 8.30) at over 175.00 were also par for the course. Photo by G.K. Callaway

For over three years, current NHRA Director of Top Fuel and Funny Car racing Ray "Engine Masters" Alley campaigned this Don Long-chassis '68 Plymouth Barracuda Funny Car out of his Garden Grove, California, "Engine Masters" High Performance Center. Originally built as a '67 Dodge Charger, an engine explosion blew the roof off the new car in the lights at Irwindale Raceway. Then, Alley and chief mechanic Dave Cole re-bodied the car into a Plymouth Barracuda, first running it with a Cole-tuned, nitro-burning injected 354 Chrysler Hemi. Then in 1968, Alley jumped up to the supercharged ranks with a blown 392 Chrysler Hemi and won the AHRA Nationals in Bristol, Tennessee. The next season, Alley stepped up to a blown 426 Hemi and ran a best of 6.61-214.00. This car was runner-up to "Jungle Clare" Sanders driving the "Jungle Jim" Liberman Chevy II at the 1969 NHRA Winternationals.

In early 1968, former AA/GS standout "Big John" Mazmanian debuted his Exhibition Engineering-built Plymouth Barracuda driven by nephew Rich Siroonian. In typical Mazmanian fashion, the car was an absolute showpiece, with its highly polished and detailed Dave Zueschel-built 392 Chrysler Hemi. In fact, the car appeared on the January 1969 cover of *Car Craft* Magazine, and *Car Craft's* editors tagged Mazmanian's new creation the *Candy 'Cuda.* On the track, Mazmanian's *'Cuda* initially ran a 7.75 at 192.00 mph with none other than former arch rival Doug "Cookie" Cook doing the tuning. Mechanical updates for the following season included a new Keith Black late-model Hemi, which propelled Mazmanian's *'Cuda* to low 7s. A top-end crash at Irwindale Raceway in the summer of 1969 demolished the *Candy 'Cuda.* Fortunately, Mazmanian already had a new Woody Gilmore car in the works. Photo by G.K. Callaway

One of the first '68 Corvette drag cars on record was the Exhibition Engineering-chassis *Mako Shark* Corvette facsimile owned by Southern California's Jim Whetton and Don Cullinan. Named after GM's highly successful Mako Shark Corvette show car and powered by a blown, fuel-burning 427 big-block Chevrolet, driver Don Cullinan (shown here at the 1968 *Hot Rod* Magazine Championship Drag Races in Riverside, California) drove the Jack Head Chevrolet-sponsored *Mako Shark* to E.T.s in the 7.60 range (best of 7.68-seconds) and terminal speeds in the high 190s. Painted in the traditional blue and white Mako Shark colors, this was one beautiful Funny Car. Photo by G.K. Callaway

In 1968, U.S. Nationals Funny Car champion and exhaust system impresario Doug Thorley signed a deal with American Motors and went Funny Car racing with a pair of Javelin-bodied Funny Cars. The first was Thorley's revolutionary rear engine *Javelin-1*, driven on various occasions by Thorley, Norm Weekly, and Bobby Hightower. The second car, *Javelin-2*, was actually the Bourgeois & Wade's Doug's Headers Logghe-chassis Corvair re-bodied into a Javelin. *Javelin-2* primarily competed on the Coca-Cola Funny Car Cavalcade of Stars circuit, which traveled throughout the Midwest and eastern seaboard. However, the team of Bourgeois & Wade's Doug's Headers occasionally ventured into national event territory, as witnessed by its appearance at the 1968 NHRA U.S. Nationals at Indianapolis Raceway Park. Bourgeois & Wade's Doug's Headers *Javelin-2* routinely ran mid 7s in the high 190s. Photo by G.K. Callaway

Not all Funny Cars were blown nitro burners. This G.K. Callaway photo was taken of Virginia racer Tom "Smoker" Smith and his *Big Red* injected, gasoline-burning Plymouth Barracuda Funny Car at Indy 1968. *Big Red* was one of a number of "budget racer" Funny Cars that competed on the eastern seaboard. In fact, in 1969 the group even formed its own traveling circuit, the East Coast Fuel Funny Car Circuit, or ECFFCC. Photo by G.K. Callaway

If there ever was a group of drag racers that was subject to the almighty-Murphy's Law, it was the trio of Joe and Frankie Pisano and former fuel-altered driver Sush Matsubara! After trading in the team's one-year-old '67 Camaro and acquiring Doug Thorley's U.S. Nationals-winning S/XS Corvair, the team appeared to be on the right track. That is, until a top-end crash at Irwindale Raceway in the summer of 1968 totaled the Pisano's new race car (with Frankie driving), as well as competitor Randy Walls' Funny Car. Then a second Corvair was ordered from Ron Scrima's Exhibition Engineering shop, only to be totaled at OCIR by newly installed driver Sush Matsubara. Joe Pisano placed yet another telephone call to Scrima, only this time he ordered a new Exhibition Engineering-built Camaro, which met an untimely end in November 1970 at the NHRA Mattel Hot Wheels Supernationals, held at Ontario Motor Speedway. Still undaunted, the team of Pisano & Matsubara placed an order with Don Long for a brand new '71 Mini Camaro, which caught fire at Fremont Raceway and completely burned the body off, although the chassis was saved. Fortunately, things settled down. In 1972, the team of Pisano & Matsubara was finally able to get through a whole season of Funny Car racing campaigning the same Long car, re-bodied into the Pisano & Matsubara Vega AA/FC, without major incident. Photo by G.K. Callaway

In June 1968, Bixby, Oklahoma's Nelson Carter and Ron Perua debuted the Logghe-chassis, Keith Black engine Imperial Kustoms Dodge Charger. According to an article in *Car Craft* Magazine, it cost $25,000 to build "the world's most expensive funny car!" In those early days, Carter had a number of top-flight drivers. After pressing business commitments forced original driver Perua to vacate the driver's seat, Steve Bovan of Blair's Speed Shop briefly jumped behind the wheel and stayed there long enough to set the OCIR Top Speed record for Funny Cars at 195.64. Right about that time, the Imperial Kustoms Dodge Charger was re-named *Super Chief* through a special contest sponsored by *Drag News*. Of course, the new name appropriately drew on Nelson Carter's Osage Indian ancestry.

Top Fuel hot shoe Dave Beebe then assumed the driving duties. I knew Beebe through my association with the *Anaheim Bulletin* newspaper. He worked around the corner at Anaheim's Cone Chevrolet, and I used to drop in there during lunch and talk drag racing with him, his brother Jerry, and line mechanic Chuck Ridgley. The weekend Beebe took over the wheel of the *Super Chief* at a race held at OCIR, he told me that he had heard some scuttlebutt in the pits that some of the Funny Car drivers were saying that a dragster driver probably couldn't handle driving a short wheelbase Funny Car. Beebe swore me to secrecy, saying that on his first run he was going to drift dangerously near the guardrail and make it look like he didn't have the car under complete control. However, he must have had second thoughts. On his first run he carried the front wheels about five feet off the starting line and ran straight as an arrow. That summer, the team of Beebe & Carter set both ends of the NHRA Funny Car record at 7.68-198.00! Photo by G.K. Callaway

In early 1969, Fort Worth, Texas, Mopar racer "Gentleman Gene" Snow really started knocking down the big numbers with his new direct-drive, Logghe-chassis, Crowerglide-equipped Keith Black-engine Dodge Charger. Both Snow and Tommy Grove are credited with being the first Funny Car drivers to break the magical 200-mph barrier, within a matter of days of each other. Here we see Snow in action at the 1969 OCIR Manufacturer's Funny Car Team Championships, where he ran 205 mph. In 1970, Snow set the AHRA record with a more compact "Mini Charger" body installed on the same chassis, clocking a 7.13-213.27 mph. For his efforts, he was voted *Drag News* "Funny Car Driver of the Year." Photo By G.K. Callaway

Tommy Grove's awesome Shedlick-bodied, Logghe-chassis *Going Thing* 427 SOHC Mach-1 Mustang AA/FC was the other machine credited with having broken the magical 200-mph barrier, at 201 mph. This car was absolutely awesome to watch. Unfortunately, standout performances such as these eventually took their toll on Grove's equipment. In late summer of 1969, the *Going Thing* Mach-1 Mustang was totally destroyed by an explosive engine fire. Throughout it all, Grove remained somewhat philosophical, as is evident in an interview conducted for the February 1991 issue of *Mustang Illustrated* Magazine. "Both ("Gentleman Gene") Snow and I have been credited with having made the first 200-mph run in a Funny Car," Grove said. "This kind of pioneering exposes both the driver and his equipment to more problems than usual. Things tend to break more frequently because we leaned on our cars harder!"

In the winter of 1969, future NHRA POWERade Drag Racing multi-car team owner Don "Shoe" Schumacher and chief mechanic "Col. John" Hogan ventured westward from their home base in Morrison, Illinois, and set the drag racing world on its ear with a string of incredible West Coast performances. For example, the team set and re-set the OCIR E.T. record at 7.48, 7.41, and 7.38-seconds with their Ed Pink-engine, Logghe-chassis *Stardust* Plymouth Barracuda, which was also clocked at an incredible 202.70 mph that same evening. Performances such as these became the norm for Schumacher, who went on to win Funny Car Eliminator at the 1970 NHRA U.S. Nationals the following summer. Photo by G.K. Callaway

The inset photo is a shot of the seldom-seen red Pat Foster-driven, Mickey Thompson Mach-1 Mustang running at Riverside International Raceway in June 1969, where it was runner-up in Funny Car Eliminator against Charlie Allen's Dodge Dart in the final. Conversely, Thompson's teammate Danny "On the Gas" Ongias, who drove Mickey's blue Mach-1 car, was usually the one who ended up in the winner's circle—but not at this event. A top-end blower explosion put an end to Ongias' quest for the gold. All the oil smoke is a dead giveaway that something was woefully wrong with Ongias' Mustang. Also notice the huge crack in the middle of the windshield.

People always identify the Farkonas, Coil & Minick *Chi-Town Hustler* Dodge Charger with smoky quarter-mile burnouts, but they seldom remember that this awesome machine was just as impressive in actual head-to-head competition. This G.K. Callaway photo shows driver Pat Minick blasting off the OCIR launch pad sometime in 1969. The *Chi-Town Hustler* posted E.T.s in the low 7s with terminal speeds of 200+ mph, which were commonplace with this incredible car. Rumor is that Pat Minick is restoring this landmark Funny Car.

The Beach City Chevrolet Corvette roadster was undoubtedly one of the most beautiful Funny Cars ever built, and it was also one of the most explosive. In the summer of 1969, driver Gary Gabelich (distinguished by his plumed helmet) was running at OCIR when the engine let go in the lights and the car exploded into a huge ball of flames. With parachutes burned off and traveling at 185.00 mph, Gabelich careened off track and into the darkness, narrowly missing a couple of cars on the OCIR return road. The Beach City Chevrolet Corvette (or what was left of it) eventually came to a smoldering stop on the side of the 405 Freeway North. While Gabelich and his crew watched helplessly as the car burned to the ground, Gary received the ultimate insult: A California Highway Patrol Officer gave him a ticket for illegally parking on the freeway! Obviously, the guy must have been a rookie. Former OCIR owner Mike McKenna recently said that when challenged, the ticket was ultimately thrown out in court. Photo by G.K. Callaway

Houma, Louisiana's Leonard Hughes raced Funny Cars for a number of years locally in NHRA Division 2 with moderate success. Then in the late 1960s, Leonard teamed up with "Tugboat Paul" Candies, and the two started setting records—like Top Speed of the Meet at the U.S. Nationals in 1968 at 201.00.

My Candies & Hughes drag racing memory begins one Sunday afternoon in April 1969 at Acquasco, Maryland, where the team had just run a 7.78-197.00 with their new Don Hardy-chassis, Keith Black-engine 1969 Plymouth Barracuda flopper. After the race, I set up an appointment to shoot the 'Cuda for my new employer, *Super Stock & Drag Illustrated* magazine. The next morning, Hughes and crewman Tom "Snake" Jones met me at our Alexandria, Virginia, office. Having just moved to Alexandria from Southern California, I was not aware of the local traffic laws that governed the Washington D.C. area. As such, I blindly guided Hughes' ramp truck up the George Washington Parkway, which runs alongside the Potomac River past National Airport, totally ignorant of the fact that trucks aren't allowed on the George Washington Parkway. As we were finishing up taking pictures at a spot by the airport known as Eagle's Landing, cop cars came roaring up from all directions!

"Give me one good reason why I shouldn't throw you all in jail and impound this rig right here and now," the head cop bellowed. "Don't you know that it's against the law to drive a truck on the parkway?"

"Uh, no sir, I didn't," I responded. "You see, I just moved here from California, and these boys are from Louisiana, and well . . ."

After about 45 minutes of groveling, along with the examination of our driver's licenses, insurance papers, registrations, and you name it, we found ourselves in the middle of a police escort sandwich, on our way back to Alexandria. We didn't get cited.

Of course, the team of Candies & Hughes survived to race another day. Noteworthy event wins of 1969 included the Rockford Dragway Manufacturer's Funny Car Championship, with a 7.35-second run over Dick Loehr's Mustang. The following season, Candies & Hughes made NHRA National event history after Hughes won Funny Car Eliminator at the NHRA Gatornationals in the team's new '70 Barracuda Funny Car, defeating Larry Reyes, who was driving the old 1969 car for an all-Candies & Hughes Funny Car finale.

NHRA Division 4 Chevrolet racer (and high school girls' basketball coach) "Professor Kelly" Chadwick is captured at the 1969 NHRA U.S. Nationals at Indianapolis Raceway Park. Chadwick's Don Hardy-built, Steakley Chevrolet-sponsored '69 Camaro flopper usually competed on the Coca-Cola Funny Car Cavalcade of Stars circuit, winning a number of 200-mph matches. In later years, Chadwick returned to "door cars," competing in NHRA Pro Stock with a Chevrolet Vega. Photo by G.K. Callaway

This is "Flash Gordon" Mineo's first fuel Funny Car, which he built at home after-hours while employed as a header builder at Garden Grove, California's Jardine Headers. And he didn't just build the chassis and engine. We're also talking about the fiberglass Firebird body as well! This was the very first car feature that I photographed for Eastern Publishing Company, and it appeared in the August 1969 issue of *Super Stock & Drag Illustrated* magazine. Mineo went on to race a whole string of AA/Fuel Funny Cars successfully before moving on to build monster trucks.

This night shot was taken of "Jungle Jim" Liberman squaring off against Randy Walls' Super Nova at the 1969 OCIR Manufacturer's Funny Car Team Championships, an event Liberman won. That year, Liberman made history by being one of the first Funny Car racers to try the two-car team concept with team driver "Jungle Clare" Sanders, who rewarded his new boss by winning Funny Car Eliminator at the 1969 NHRA Winternationals. There was an East Coast car (Sanders) and a West Coast car (Liberman) although, in truth, both cars toured the entire country. And Liberman's candy blue Chevy IIs had different major sponsors. Rich Guess' Goodies Speed Shop sponsored Liberman's car, and Steve Kanuika Speed Shops sponsored Sanders' Chevy II. Both cars routinely ran in the 7.30s at 197.00. Photo by G.K. Callaway

In 1969, East Coast Funny Car racers Russell and Tony Wahlay ventured out to the NHRA Winternationals to test the waters. After all, their new Funny Car, the Logghe chassis *Warlord III* Plymouth Barracuda, was capable of running low 7s at close to 200 mph, but with a huge field entered for the NHRA Winternationals' first official Funny Car Eliminator, the Wahlays found the going tougher than expected. Photo by G.K. Callaway

First you go this a-way and then you go that a-way! That's the way it was at the 1970 Mattel Hot Wheels Supernationals.—
The burnout box, which in truth was the beginning of the pit road entrance at Ontario Motor Speedway (OMS), was located
approximately 15 to 20 degrees off-center to the actual pit entrance road, or in this case, the drag strip. Of course, this
wreaked havoc with many of the top name Funny Car drivers in attendance, like "Big John" Mazmanian and hot shoe Rich
Siroonian, who found himself playing the old road racer in the burnout box game.

This shot of Fritz Callier, driving the Callier, Kristek & Cortinnas CKC Chevy II and racing "Big John" Mazmanian, was taken at the 1970 OCIR Manufacturer's Funny Car Team Championships. Although the CKC Racing Team boasted first-class equipment, like the Don Hardy Race Cars-constructed Chevy II, and could step-up at any given time, they rarely ventured outside NHRA Division 4, preferring to stay close to home. In the two years that the team raced this particular car (they had a total of three), it was powered by a blown Chevrolet and ran in the 7.20s at 190 mph. Then they switched out the Chevy for a Chrysler and ran 7 flat at 200 mph.

This shot of Don "Shoe" Schumacher was taken in the burnout box at the 1971 NHRA U.S. Nationals. Who do you think won this race, Schumacher or crewman Jerry Irving?

In 1971, car owner Harry M. Schmidt and driver Richard Tharp fielded the *Blue Max III*, which was built by *Car Craft* Magazine All-Star Drag Team chassis builder "Lil' John" Buttera. The new *Blue Max III* was as beautiful as it was fast, with its candy blue and white paint, canard wings (which were later outlawed), and plenty of spit and polish. The car was capable of running 6.40 at 220+ mph at will.

The *Hawaiian* Charger started out life as Ray "Engine Masters" Alley's "Lil' John" Buttera-built '71 Mach-1 Mustang Funny Car that was driven by both Alley and Dave Beebe. Then, in 1972 the car was converted to the Engine Masters Dodge Charger and driven by future NHRA-Winston Funny Car and Top Fuel World Champion Kenny Bernstein in the runner-up spot to Raymond Beadle driving the Don "Shoe" Schumacher Vega at the 1972 NHRA Winternationals. After Roland "The Hawaiian" Leong's Buttera-built *Hawaiian* was stolen, Leong purchased the car from Alley and screwed driver Gordia Bonin behind the wheel of the "new" *Hawaiian*. Both Bonin and Ron Colson drove this chassis, first as a Charger and later as the Chevrolet Monza-bodied *Hawaiian*. All clear on that?

*H*awaiian driver Butch Maas lights 'em up at the 1971 NHRA Winternationals. In its heyday, the Logghe Stage III chassis, Keith Black-powered *Hawaiian* AA/FC was considered one of the most beautiful cars in the Eliminator, running 6.50s at 220.00.

As you can see from this late afternoon shot of Arnie Behling driving the Ramchargers' second Dodge Challenger AA/FC at Ontario Motor Speedway, the burnout box was still placed cockeyed to the OMS starting line, and the Funny Cars were still making like SCCA racers. Mind you, though, none of us photographers ever complained!

I've always liked this shot of Gary Bolger driving the Richter Automotive-sponsored *Gold Digger* Dodge Charger, because of the unique smoke pattern coming off the tires and the way you can catch a glimpse of daylight under the front wheel.

The Exhibition Engineering-chassis King Camaro AA/FC driven by Dean La Pole and wrenched by Dan Geare was reputed to have been equipped with a trick set of 16-spark-plug cylinder heads. As such, the car had a few unique quirks. The Camaro obviously sounded different than other blown fuel-burning Chevrolets, and when it ran at night, the King Camaro belched out some incredible header flames. Unfortunately, twin spark plugs also meant a twin ignition, and that meant twice the headaches.

In the early 1970s, San Antonio "Texicans" Johnny Valadez and partners Frank Altamirano and David Guerrero (together with mechanic Bobby Rex) raced this red, white, and green Don Hardy Camaro called the *Mexican Revolution*. Although the *Mexican Revolution* was primarily raced around the Texas, Oklahoma, and New Mexico area, running a best of 7.01 at 214.00 mph, it ventured up to the Midwest at least once that we know of, where it was runner-up to none other than Tom "Mongoose" McEwen at the AHRA-Kansas City Grand American event.

In 1970, the Pacific Northwestern Funny Car team of Ed "Ace" McCulloch and Art "The Whip" Whipple (later from Whipple Supercharger's fame) lost their '70 Plymouth Duster in a freak trailer fire and were hard-pressed to fulfill lucrative booking engagements. Then along came Fresno, California's "Mr. Ed" Wills, who had just taken delivery of this Dick Fletcher-chassis Plymouth Barracuda AA/FC. Art and Ed installed one of their blown Chrysler engines in the 'Cuda, and the interim Funny Car team of Whipple, McCulloch & Wills made its official debut at the AHRA Winternationals. In later years, Whipple (who eventually married Wills' daughter) teamed up with his father-in-law on a pair of Whipple & Mr. Ed Plymouth Satellite Funny Cars driven by the likes of "Hollywood Kelly" Brown, Bobby Rowe, and Dave Beebe.

San Rafael, California's Mike "Hippie" Mitchell, drag racing's self-proclaimed "World's Fastest Hippie," with his last race car, a '72 Sid Waterman-engine Plymouth Barracuda AA/FC, which ran mid 6s at 220 mph. Considered somewhat controversial for his political views, Mitchell got himself into hot water with the NHRA over a political message about then-President Richard M. Nixon that he had lettered across the rear spoiler of his Funny Car. It read "Impeach Nixon!" but the "x" in Nixon was replaced with a Nazi swastika. At Pomona that year the NHRA was less than impressed. Here we see Mitchell staging up against Sush Matsubara at an OCIR night race in 1972.

Chevrolet Funny Car superstar Dick Harrell gets up close and personal at the 1971 Lions Associated Drag Strip AHRA Grand American race driving the Harrell & Christophersen, Don Hardy-chassis Chevrolet Vega, which was reported to be the first of its kind. Powered by a Howard's Cams-equipped 426 Hemi, the Vega ran high 6s at 200 mph.

In January 1972, La Mirada, California, fireman "Big Jim" Dunn debuted his new Woody Gilmore-Race Car Engineering chassis rear-engine Plymouth Barracuda AA/FC at the Lions Associated Drag Strip Grand American race. Dunn worked hard at making the rear-engine concept work, making running changes along the way. Things finally began to pay off at the close of the 1972 racing season, when Dunn won the Funny Car Eliminator title at the Mattel Hot Wheels Supernationals over Pat Foster driving the Barry Setzer Vega. That was the only time in NHRA history that a rear engine Funny Car would win a national event.

   More running changes were made the following season. Dunn swapped out his tried-and-true 392 Hemi for a blown 426 late-model Hemi. He also swapped out the body, changing over to a lighter weight, metal-flake blue Mr. Ed Plymouth Barracuda facsimile (inset photo). That year, the Dunn & Reath 'Cuda won the AHRA Funny Car Championship.

Undoubtedly, one of drag racing's most popular non-drivers from the 1970s was "Jungle Pam" Hardy, the one-time girlfriend of the Funny Car icon "Jungle Jim" Liberman. The story goes that one day while Liberman was out chasing parts, he spied this statuesque 5-feet-6-inch young lady walking down the street in Westchester, Pennsylvania. The rest is history. Up until that time, Hardy had never been to a drag race, but the ever-persuasive Liberman convinced her that there was nothing more exciting than the sound of a fuel Funny Car firing up to make a run. Or as Liberman used to say in his Raceway Park radio spots, "Drag racing is f-a-r-r-r-r out!"

Hardy's comely looks quickly endeared her to Liberman's fans all across the country, and she was cheered wildly as she backed him up in his tracks after his patented 1,000-foot burnouts. In fact, at one time I would say that Hardy's popularity almost rivaled that of Liberman himself. Realizing this, Liberman seized the opportunity and increased his booking fees. He offered two packages: the base price without Pam backing him up, and the deluxe package, which included Hardy. As there were a lot of people who admired Pam for her impressive physical "architecture," there weren't too many promoters who went for the base price. As well, anyone who took the time to get to really know Hardy quickly realized she was an extremely articulate and well-educated woman with a heart the size of Texas.

The '71 to '73 Ford Mustangs made great Funny Cars. Aside from the record setting *Blue Max* of Harry Schmidt and Richard Tharp, there were other Mustang standouts in Funny Car Eliminator that included:

Eight time NHRA Northwest Division 6 Top Fuel champion Jerry "King" Ruth, shown here at OCIR racing Keeling & Clayton's Pinto.

Eighteen-year-old Billy "Waco Willy" Meyer driving his Success Motivation Institute (SMI) S&R chassis, Sid Waterman-engine *Motivator* Mustang AA/FC at the IHRA Springnationals in Bristol, Tennessee.

Harlan Thompson driving Jerry Batles *Tom and Jerry* Mustang at the 1972 NHRA U.S. Nationals in Indianapolis.

NHRA Division 3 racer Dale Creasy driving the Creasy Brothers *Tyrant* Mustang AA/FC at Green Valley, Texas.

Lew Arrington driving the Logghe chassis *Brutus* Mustang, racing Charlie Therwanger in "Big Mike" Burkhart's Chevrolet Camaro at the *Cars* Magazine Meet in Atco, New Jersey, during the summer of 1972.

Tommy Grove's Lindblad chassis *Kong* Mustang, which was one of the fastest Mustangs in the nation at 6.42-227.00, seen here at the AHRA World Finals at Baylands Raceway in Fremont, California.

Gary Burgin's "Lil' John" Buttera-built Vega AA/FC (Brasket & Burgin) that set the AHRA Funny Car E.T. record at 6.99-seconds.

Jim Paoli, the 1970 and 1971 NHRA Division 3 Top Fuel champion, went Funny Car racing with this Woody Gilmore-chassis Chevrolet Vega.

The Mike Kaase-built, Donovan engine *Blackhawk* Vega owned by Mike Young was another entry into the "Vega Wars." This machine primarily competed on the AHRA Midwest circuit with mixed results.

In 1972, Mt. Clemens, Michigan, metalsmith Al Bergler (Bergler Race Car Bodies) fielded this flamed, Keith Black Chrysler-powered Chevrolet Vega AA/FC *Motown Shaker*. Bergler's Vega ran a best of 6.14-240.00. Al won Best Appearing Car at Gainesville 1972, while simultaneously burning the car to the ground racing against Pat Foster and Barry Setzer.

Future *Hawaiian* Funny Car hot shoe and NHRA staffer Gordie Bonin burst onto the national scene driving Canadian Ron Hodgson's *Pacemaker* Chevrolet Vega, seen here in action at the 1972 NHRA U.S. Nationals.

In 1972, former gasser racer Jim "Fireball" Shores (Phillips & Shores) rolled out the Ed Pink engine *Fireball Vega*, which primarily competed on the eastern seaboard.

GM's new compact economy car, the Chevrolet Vega, made a far better race car than it ever did a street car. This x-ray shot of the "Lil' John" Buttera-built Radici & Wise Vega AA/FC (considered state of the art for its day) clearly shows all of its internal working components.

This overhead view of Jim Green's *Green Elephant* Chevrolet Vega was taken at Indianapolis 1973 from the Hurst Performance crossover bridge. Frank Hall drove the car.

Here's "Big Mike" Burkhart's driver Charlie Therwanger boiling the hides at OCIR. What's interesting about this car is the fact that it's still Chevrolet powered! The car ran a career best of 6.98-seconds.

This shot of East Coast Funny Car racer Al Segrini driving Kosty Ivanoff's '72 Vega was taken at the NHRA Summernationals at Raceway Park in Old Bridge Township, New Jersey. This was a time exposure photo with the lens left open while taking advantage of all the other photographers' multiple flashes around me.

In 1972, Don "Rack" Rackeman and Bob Cashler put together the *Wonder Wagon* twin-Vega panel-car Funny Car project with ITT Continental Bakeries as the primary sponsor. Glenn "Groundshakers" Way and "Hollywood Kelly" Brown drove these cars. Ultimately, Don "Shoe" Schumacher picked up the proverbial "ball" and ran with the Wonder Bread sponsorship after a legal battle between the sponsor and the original contractors. Unfortunately, the entire program was canceled when the term of the contract expired.

Probably the baddest Vega in all of drag racing was Barry Setzer's, driven by Pat Foster and seen here in action at the NHRA Summernationals, where Foster won. This car ran as quick as 6.29-seconds at 228.00.

This twilight shot of "Lil' John" Lombardo and his Donovan-engine, S&R-chassis Vega was taken at OCIR in the summer of 1972. In its later life, this car became the *L.A. Hooker* Vega, which was briefly driven by none other than John "Brute" Force. I vividly remember one night at OCIR when Force went into a giant wheelie off the starting line and hooked a hard right, almost knocking a handful of photographers off of our stepladders!

In 1972, Venice, California's Revell, Inc. launched the Revell Drag Racing Team, which started out with members Tony "Loner" Nancy, Keeling & Clayton, "Gentleman Gene" Snow, "Jungle Jim" Liberman, and Ed "Ace" McCulloch. Simultaneously, the company released a series of incredibly detailed 1/25-scale and 1/16-scale model kits of these famous race cars. The Revell Drag Racing Team quickly expanded its sphere of influence, taking on new members "Da Revell Fast Guys" Kuhl & Olson; "Wild Willie" Borsch, a.k.a., "Revell's Wild Man"; Mickey Thompson; Custom Body Enterprises; Hanna & Mundet, the "Revell Eastern Raider"; Butch "The Revell California Flash" Leal; and numerous others. This photo was taken in 1973 at my Van Nuys, California, photo studio of Revell, Inc. drag racing consultant and future NHRA Motorsports Museum co-founder/curator John Zendejas, aka "John Zenda," for an article I was preparing for *Cars* magazine on the birth of a Revell Models drag race car. It was definitely a fun time!

This shot of "Gentleman Gene" Snow's first (Revell-sponsored) Dodge Charger was taken late one afternoon at OCIR. The "Revell Snowman" and team driver Jake Johnston had a two-car fire burnout scheduled for the cover of *Hot Rod* magazine, and Snow was "practicing."

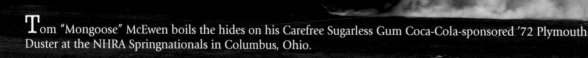

Tom "Mongoose" McEwen boils the hides on his Carefree Sugarless Gum Coca-Cola-sponsored '72 Plymouth Duster at the NHRA Springnationals in Columbus, Ohio.

Things didn't go to well for NHRA Division 7 Funny Car racer Jeff Courtie at the 1973 NHRA Supernationals held at Ontario Motor Speedway (OMS). In the process of qualifying his beautiful candy blue Plymouth Barracuda (best of 7.03-seconds), Jeff popped a blower mid-track and blew the 'Cuda's J&E Fiberglass body shell into lots of little 'Cuda pieces! Courtie later re-bodied this car into a Mustang II and ran it for a couple more seasons.

Local NHRA Division 7 racer Mike Halloran trips OCIR's finish line lights in his '73 Dodge Charger, which is about a half a car length ahead of Bays & Rupert's Plymouth Barracuda AA/FC.

In 1971, Chicago auto dealer "Mr. Norm" Krauss' Grand Spaulding Dodge dealership and Gary Dyer parked the *Mr. Norm Mini Charger* and rolled out their new Romeo Palamadis-built Dodge Challenger AA/FC, which continued in Mr. Norm's winning tradition.

From 1972 to 1974, Don "The Snake" Prudhomme raced this "Lil John" John Buttera-built Plymouth Barracuda AA/FC, first as the Carefree Sugarless Gum car (1972) and then as the U.S. Army 'Cuda after Prudhomme's new U.S. Army-sponsored Buttera-built "lay down" Chevrolet Vega turned out be a huge disappointment during 1973 and 1974. Prudhomme's U.S. Army 'Cuda ran a best of 6.33-seconds at the rain-delayed final at Indy 1974 against runner-up Billy "Waco Willy" Meyer.

In 1974, former Don "Shoe" Schumacher team driver Raymond Beadle, who was runner-up in Funny Car Eliminator at the 1973 NHRA Winternationals, coaxed *Blue Max* owner Harry Schmidt out of retirement, and the two teamed up to introduce the latest in a long line of *Blue Max* AA/Fuel Funny Cars. *New Blue* was based on a Tony Casarez Race Cars chassis and featured Ed Pink power and a J&E Fiberglass Mustang II body. Tuned by Harry Schmidt (with assistance from "Waterbed Fred" Miller) and driven by Raymond Beadle, the *Blue Max* Mustang II reeled off 6.40s with ease. These photos were taken for *Drag Racing* magazine at Texas Stadium, which is home to another Texas tradition, the Dallas Cowboys.

The *Super Duster* AA/FC of Taylor & Wolf with Gary Henderson behind the wheel was driven to numerous NHRA Division 2 wins. The *Super Duster* was one of a number of Funny Cars that originated between the mid 1960s and the late 1970s out of Memphis, Tennessee's Coleman-Taylor Enterprises.

Land-speed record holder and female motorsports icon Paula "Miss STP" Murphy campaigned a number of Funny Cars over the years, but her last car, this Jack Bynum-tuned, late-model Hemi-powered, Romeo Palamides Duster (sponsored by STP Oil Filters) was by far her best. Murphy divided her time between match racing and running the STP Duster on both the AHRA and IHRA circuits, where she ran in the high 6s at 220 mph. Alas, the high cost of racing in the mid 1970s pretty much put an end to her Funny Car racing days, but she continued racing all kinds of different cars, ranging from land speed record cars to sport compact cars. Murphy was recently honored for her contributions to the sport at the 2004 California Hot Rod Reunion.

No Funny Car section is complete without some BB/FC action, so let's start with Joe Amato. Yes, this was the car future NHRA-Winston Top Fuel World Champion (1984, 1988, 1990, 1991, and 1992) Amato started out with. In its heyday, Joe's S&W Race Cars *Keystone 'Kuda* BB/FC was the class of the field on the eastern seaboard, with numerous circuit wins and event titles to its credit.

Lorry Azevedo and studio musician John Kinsel ventured forth from San Rafael, California, in 1972 to knock 'em dead at the NHRA Springnationals at Raceway Park. Azevedo was the class of the field in NHRA Competition Eliminator with the team's Woody Gilmore-chassis, Keith Black-engine *Drummer* Camaro A/FC running an incredible string of low 7s (7.35, 7.37, and 7.50) with a best of 165.44 to win the Eliminator class, forever silencing East Coast skeptics about the validity of injected Funny Cars out on the "left coast!"

West Coast Funny Car racer Ken Veney set both the NHRA A/FC E.T. and MPH record at 7.04-191.89 in his Ken Cox chassis *Veney's Vega*. Then Veney switched over to blown alcohol and ran a 6.70-second to win Pro Comp at the 1976 NHRA Summernationals.

In the summer of 1974, "Wild Wilfred" Boutillier and his Ken Cox-chassis *Wilfred's Chevron* BB/FC became the first Funny Car in the sixes, recording a 6.98-second run at the Irwindale Grand Premiere after qualifying earlier in the day with a 7.10! Boutillier's time stood as an official track record and sent a message to all the boys on the East Coast that these weren't popcorn times they were turning out west! Incidentally, this very shot was taken on that record-breaking 6.98-second run, and it was used on the cover of the April 1974 issue of *Drag Racing* magazine.

The Zig & Dietz *Hawkeye* Chevrolet Vega BB/FC driven by Frank "Hawk" Harris was another strong-running Top Alcohol Funny Car from NHRA Division 7. The Ken Cox-chassis Vega used pure Chevrolet power to propel it to a best of 6.85-199.99 mph.

"We could never break 200 mph," said magneto guru Don Zig. "We must have run 199.99 at least 50 times!"

Noteworthy performances included a number of NHRA Division 7 wins, along with a runner-up spot to Adams & Enriquez at the 1975 March Meet.

Years before "Bad Brad" Anderson's siblings Randy and Shelley made their mark in both Top Fuel and Funny Car racing, old dad was out there givin' 'em hell with this BA-engine Dodge Dart BB/FC that ran mid 6s at 200+ mph.

And here's the man himself, "AA/Dale" Armstrong! The Canadian transplant had a banner year in 1975. Armstrong's Donovan 417 top alcohol engine development program was paid off with really big dyno numbers, and he had a brand new Mike Kaase-constructed Plymouth Satellite built in which to install one of these ground-pounding alcohol-burning Chryslers. The Armstrong & Foust *Alcoholic* BB/FC flat got with the program. Noteworthy performances included the NHRA-Winston Division 7 Championship, along with wins at Indy and the NHRA-Winston Finals (where Dale cinched the championship), as well as runner-up at Englishtown. In NHRA-legal trim, Armstrong's *Alcoholic* recorded a best of 6.51-202.00. However, in match race trim, the *Alcoholic* ran as quick as 6.48-seconds. "That car was a natural," commented Armstrong. "It was the best ride I ever had. One of the things I really used to enjoy was qualifying against the AA/FCs at local shows and running away with all the marbles, which happened on more than one occasion!"

This wild-looking shot was taken of Tom Hoover and his 1974 Plymouth Satellite AA/FC at the 1974 NHRA World Finals held at Ontario Motor Speedway, just seconds before the skies clouded up and drenched everyone in sight.

I guess you might call this the "Battle of the Satellites," a classic confrontation between "Nitro Twig" Ziegler (Pizza Haven) and "Hollywood Kelly" Brown in the *Mr. Ed* car at the U.S. Nationals. Judging from what's going on in this picture, it's easy to guess who won the race.

These photos of Don "Shoe" Schumacher and his *Revell Super Shoe* 1974 "Lil' John" Buttera Vega AA/FC aren't what they appear to be. First of all, that's Dale Pulde hiding behind the facemask and posing for my camera, as Schumacher was laid up at home recuperating from back surgery. However, no one was the wiser, as both Pulde and the Vega appeared on the May 1974 cover of *Super Stock & Drag Illustrated* magazine.

In the mid 1970s, former NHRA Division 1 gasser and fuel-altered racers Charlie "Filthy 40" Hill and Bob "Bad Habit" Parmer fielded the *Bad Habit* Ford Pinto AA/FC. Shown here in action at Raceway Park, Parmer and Hill routinely ran high 6s at 220.00 mph.

In the mid 1970s, Joe Pisano and Sush Matsubara overcame their jinx and campaigned this Revell-sponsored Chevrolet Vega without major incident. Maybe it was the change in colors, but the Ed Pink-engine Revell Vega routinely ran in the 6.50-second zone at around 220 mph. P&M would never realize a national event win, but they nonetheless always seemed to be in the hunt.

OPPOSITE TOP: Ed "Ace" McCulloch's Ed Pink-engine *Revellution* Dodge Demon was one of NHRA-Winston National event competition's strongest running entries, with a total of 18 victories to his credit beginning with the 1971 U.S. Nationals at Indy.

OPPOSITE: Tom Prock successfully piloted a number of Custom Body Enterprises Dodges throughout the mid 1970s that were owned by Utica, New York's Fred Castronovo. The Jaime Sarte-built, Keith Black-engine *Utica Flash* Dodge Dart was tuned to a best of 6.40-seconds at 220+ mph by Steve Bernd. Accomplishments included winning the big 1964 Funny Car Meet in Epping, New Hampshire.

Fred Goeske's mid 1970s switch from Mopar-bodied cars to this Chevrolet Vega came and went with relatively little fanfare. However, Goeske experienced one anxious moment at the 1974 March Meet in Bakersfield, California, when his new mount decided to hook a hard right coming off the starting line against Mike "Hippie" Mitchell, forcing Goeske to play road racer for just a little while.

With the release of the new "Mr. Ed" Wills-produced Plymouth Satellite fiberglass Funny Car bodies in 1972, the team of (Tim "Chops") Beebe & (Dick) Rosberg built themselves this beautiful new Dennis Watson-chassis *Fighting Irish* Plymouth Satellite Funny Car, which they primarily campaigned throughout the Midwest. Then it was back to Top Fuel dragsters for Beebe (Beebe & Murphy) and on to jet cars for Rosberg.

In 1974, Al Segrini vacated the driver's seat of Kosty Ivanoff's Vega and went to work for ATI's Jim Beattie driving the *Black Magic* Chevrolet Vega AA/FC. This car was a class act, and it won a bunch of "Best Appearing" awards at events. Moreover, the car performed exceptionally well, running in the mid 6s at 220+ mph. Of course, ATI was renowned in the torque converter, harmonic balancer, and high-performance transmission business on the East Coast.

Ron "Snag" O'Donnell is off and running behind the wheel of the *Damn Yankee* '74 Chevrolet Vega at the U.S. Nationals in Indy. O'Donnell was the renowned driver of such rides as the Dennison, Arlasky & Knox AA/FA, the Chapman Camaro, and "Captain Chris" Karamesines' Plymouth Barracuda FC. But the *Damn Yankee* was all O'Donnell's— lock, stock, barrel, and bills!

Fuel-altered handler Dennis Geisler must have felt right at home at Pomona driving Bert Berniker's *Hindsight* rear-engine Plymouth Duster AA/FC. After a hard leave off the starting line, the Duster climbed up on the gear and went into a wild wheel stand, flipping over at the eighth mile and separating the J&E Fiberglass body from its chassis. Sadly, the car was totaled, but luckily Geisler was unhurt.

Bob Pickett is seen here piloting Pete Everett's Don Long-chassis, Keith Black-engine *Pete's Lil' Demon* AA/FC at Irwindale Raceway in the summer of 1975. The team primarily competed in NHRA Division 7 points championship meets and locally at tracks like Irwindale, Lions Associated Drag Strip, and OCIR, where they experienced sporadic success.

A number of racers adapted Mr. Ed Plymouth Satellite fiberglass Funny Car body shells to suit their own purposes. For example, Jim "Holy Smokes" Murphy built a Plymouth Road Runner out of one, and Roger "Color Me Gone" Lindamood built this Dodge Charger, which he primarily ran on the Coca-Cola Funny Car Cavalcade of Stars circuit.

In 1975, Ron Hodgson, Gordie Bonin, and Jerry Verhuel came out with the Chassis Components-built *Bubble Up Monza* AA/FC, shown here in competition at Irwindale Raceway. Low 6-second times and high 220s were Bonin's calling card.

Is this the world's tallest saguaro cactus or the world's smallest Funny Car? I'm no expert on cacti, but this has to be a record setter. I discovered this massive saguaro near famed Beeline Dragway while searching for a location to shoot John Luna's Vega Funny Car for a *Cars* magazine photo feature. The next day, Luna competed with his Don Long-chassis, Sid Waterman-engine Vega at the 1975 AHRA Winternationals. John's car was capable of running 6.70 at 220+ mph and was primarily match raced.

Here's the dynamic duo from the Buckeye State. In 1971, renown Funny Car pilot Dale "Snail" Emery and high-performance parts retailer Jeg Coughlin (JEG'S) got together on this Logghe-chassis Camaro AA/FC, which had the dubious distinction of exploding an engine in the lights and subsequently blowing the fiberglass body all to bits at the 1971 U.S. Nationals. However, the team would return with a vengeance and a brand new Jaime Sarte Camaro at the 1972 NHRA Winternationals and redeem itself by winning Funny Car Eliminator, giving Coughlin his first NHRA national event win.

This is expatriated *Blue Max* driver Richard Tharp behind the wheel of the Huff & Guasco Soapy Sales-Dyna Gym-sponsored "Lil' John" Buttera lay-down '74 Dodge Dart AA/FC competing at the Bakersfield March Meet. The association was short-lived.

Former NHRA Division 4 Funny Car title holder (1976 and 1977) and 1977 NHRA Cajun Nationals Funny Car champ John White and his *Houston Hustler '81* Corvette AA/FC are seen here in action at OCIR. This was the last of a long line of *Houston Hustler* Funny Cars that White campaigned, and the car ran a best of 6.04 with an incredible 242.00 top-end charge at the 1983 U.S Nationals.

This photo session for *Drag Racing USA* Magazine featuring Dennis Fowler's *Sundance* Chevrolet Monza happened on the *Blazing Saddles* set at Warner Brothers Pictures, circa 1975. The S&R-chassis, Sid Waterman-engine *Sundance* Monza was driven by Russell Long and crewed by Lindsay Duyzon.

As the 1970s came to a close, the Mopar body of choice was the new subcompact Dodge Charger. Shown here competing at the NHRA Winternationals in Pomona is Ron Colson wheeling Roland "The Hawaiian" Leong's *Hawaiian* Dodge Charger-bodied AA/FC, which was sponsored by King's Hawaiian Bread.

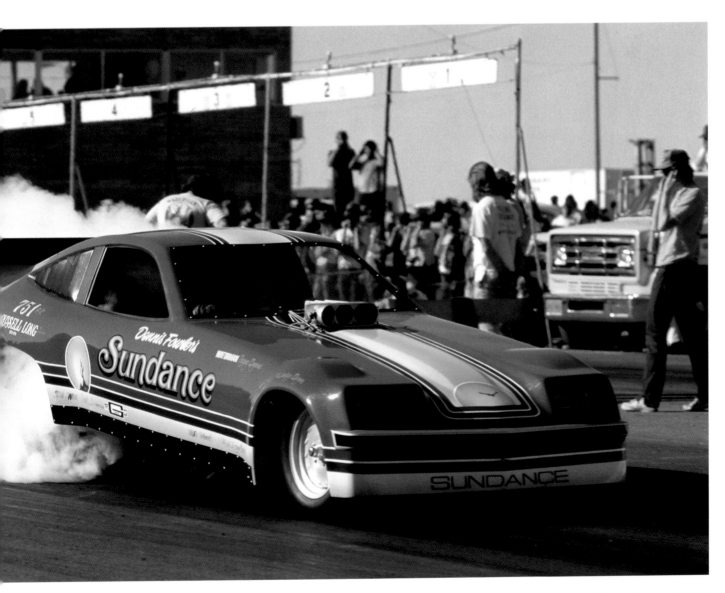

This black and white wheel stand sequence of the Mike Kaase-built *Iron Mike* Dodge Charger was taken at the 1984 NHRA U.S. Nationals at Indy. As you can see, things got a little out of hand upon re-entry, as the body appeared to have a mind of its own.

Former Top Fuel hot shoe Jody Smart went Funny Car racing in 1984 with this Gary Burgin-tuned Pontiac Firebird. However, as you can see from this photo taken at the NHRA Winternationals, things went slightly awry.

In 1984, John "Brute" Force made the best business decision in his life when he hired Austin Coil away from the *Chi-Town Hustler* team. Coil's incredible mechanical expertise and creative mind have allowed Force to capture more than 120 national event victories and 13 NHRA-Winston and NHRA POWERade World Championships.

Chapter 4

GASSERS & ALTEREDS

The Hawkins, Webster & McLeod *15 OZ* Chrysler-powered '34 Ford five-window coupe competed in CF/AC and Fuel Altered Eliminator with Lyle Webster driving. The '34 Ford recorded a top-end speed of 157.61 mph. Challenger Automotive's Jim Kirby is currently restoring this Hawkins, Webster & McLeod *15 OZ*, and it will be driven at the nostalgia races by none other than Gary Southern. Photo by G.K. Callaway

Pomona, California's C&W Motor Parts and Hooker Headers sponsored the West Coast-based '41 Willys B/Gasser of Greer & Barber. The car ran in the 10-second range with power coming from an injected small-block Chevrolet. Photo by G.K. Callaway

NHRA Pro Stock racer and Central California trucking magnate Bob Panella started out racing this beautiful candy apple red '41 Willys pickup truck built by Al Del Porto. Powered by a Bob "Bones" Balogh-built, supercharged 327 Chevrolet and driven by Joe Morris, the Willys competed in the BB/GS class with reasonable success. This photo was taken of Panella & Morris in action at Half Moon Bay around 1965. Bob Panella and driver Ken Dondero went on to campaign the fabled Panella Trucking BB/GS Anglia, which set the NHRA BB/GS record at 9.74 and won the 1969 NHRA Springnationals. Photo by G.K. Callaway

I originally became a "Big John" Mazmanian fan way back in the early 1960s when John used to race a candy apple red BB Modified Sports (BB/MSP) '61 Corvette. Then in late 1963, I was delighted to learn that Maz had just debuted an all-new '41 Willys gasser built by Ron Scrima/Pat Foster/B&M Automotive, and driven by Bob "Bones" Balogh.

Originally powered by the same 338-ci blown small-block Chevrolet engine that had powered Mazmanian's Corvette, the new Willys went out and obliterated the BB/GS record. But there were bigger fish to fry. In the winter of 1963, Mazmanian installed a 466-ci Dave Zueschel-assembled blown Chrysler Hemi that placed the Willys in the AA/GS class, which in recent years had been dominated by the team of Stone, Woods & Cook. With both cars running right on the NHRA National record, and in some cases below it, it was only a matter of time before the two would face each other for the title "King of the Gassers."

This battle for gasser supremacy raged on for two whole years, reaching epic proportions due in part to the fact that both teams' cam grinders, Jack Engle (Stone, Woods & Cook) and Ed Iskenderian (Mazmanian) happened to be having a war of their own. Performance claims and insults, both real and contrived, were traded back and forth in Drag News and National DRAGSTER each week once automotive cartoonist Pete Millar orchestrated the legendary Big June versus Pebble, Pulp & Chef series of advertorials.

Probably one of the most memorable Stone, Woods & Cook versus Mazmanian confrontations happened at Lions Associated Drag Strip (LADS) in the summer of 1964, where 10,500 fans gathered to see these two gasser greats square off against each other in a best (E.T.) of two match race. Both teams warmed up with runs in the low 10s, (10.11 Cook) and high 9s, (9.99 Mazmanian). In round one, Balogh, in Mazmanian's red '41 Willys, was out first, recording a 9.96-143.06 to Doug "Cookie" Cook's quicker but losing 9.91-144.59. However, the shoe was on the other foot in round two, when Cook hammered out a 9.93-144.22 to Balogh's 9.99-141.06.

Here's my drag racing memory: In my junior year of high school my English instructor, Mr. John Rowe, assigned the class to write a report on a topical subject or current event. Having attended this very match race at Lions and fully armed with a fresh copy of the November 1964 issue of Drag Racing Magazine, which carried coverage from that event, I sat down and wrote my report, paraphrasing what I had read in the magazine. My instructor was less than impressed with both the subject content and the actual writing. I received an "F!" Photo by G.K. Callaway

Ohio racer Fred Hurst campaigned a number of gassers during his career, all with late-model Chrysler Hemis. Here's Hurst's Hemi-powered '41 Willys A/Gasser in action at the 1967 NHRA U.S. Nationals, where he won the class running a 9.81-141.73. This was one beautiful car. Photo by G.K. Callaway

This is Northern California gasser racer Mike "Hippie" Mitchell in his pre-hippie days driving the Chuck Finders-built, Hamberis & Mitchell BB/GS, George Linton Chevrolet-powered '33 Willys coupe at Lions Associated Drag Strip, circa 1965. Of course, this is the same Willys that Mitchell repainted in psychedelic red, white, and blue, installed a blown 392 Chrysler in, and dominated the So Cal AA/GS scene in 1967 and 1968, just prior to building his infamous AA/GS Corvette roadster. Photo by G.K. Callaway

Here's a classic match-up between Ron Nunes' Chrysler-powered (yeah, it still says "Oldsmobile" on the hood) '41 Willys AA/GS against Bob "Bones" Balogh in the Bones, Dubach & Pisano AA/GS '33 Willys coupe at the *Hot Rod Magazine* Championship Drag Races at Riverside International Raceway in June 1966. Judging from the photo, it's pretty easy to guess who won. Photo by G.K. Callaway

Here's an even earlier photo of Ron Nunes and his Oldsmobile-powered '41 Willys at Half Moon Bay, California, where the car ran as a BB/GS and bombed the record at 9.94-seconds. According to *Supercharged Gas Coupes* author Don Montgomery, Nunes was the only guy to have his blown-gas record (which had been improved by almost a full second) erased by the NHRA because it was too good! Photo by G.K. Callaway

Ron Bizio's beautiful candy blue *Beaver Shot* '33 Willys pickup was a dominant force in late 1960s Southern California gasser racing. Originally built by Chuck Finders and powered by a blown Chevrolet racing under the *Tall Texan* name, the truck was later updated by Steve Pflueger (S&R Race Cars) with a Dave Braskett-built blown Chrysler. Prior to its sale in 1968, Bizio ran a best of 8.43-166.35 with the truck. The Ron Bizio '33 Willys has since been restored and is now owned by Tom Willford.

The little Anglias and Ford Prefects were starting to make themselves known in NHRA and AHRA drag racing by the mid 1960s. The *Super Six* was a Ford-powered H/Gas Anglia that ran 11.60s. Photo by G.K. Callaway

The *Royal Kahuna* was a Chrysler Hemi-powered BB/GS Anglia from the Midwest and featured a state-of-the-art chassis, complete with a tubbed and narrowed rear end. The car is seen here in competition at the 1969 NHRA U.S. Nationals at Indy. Photo by G.K. Callaway

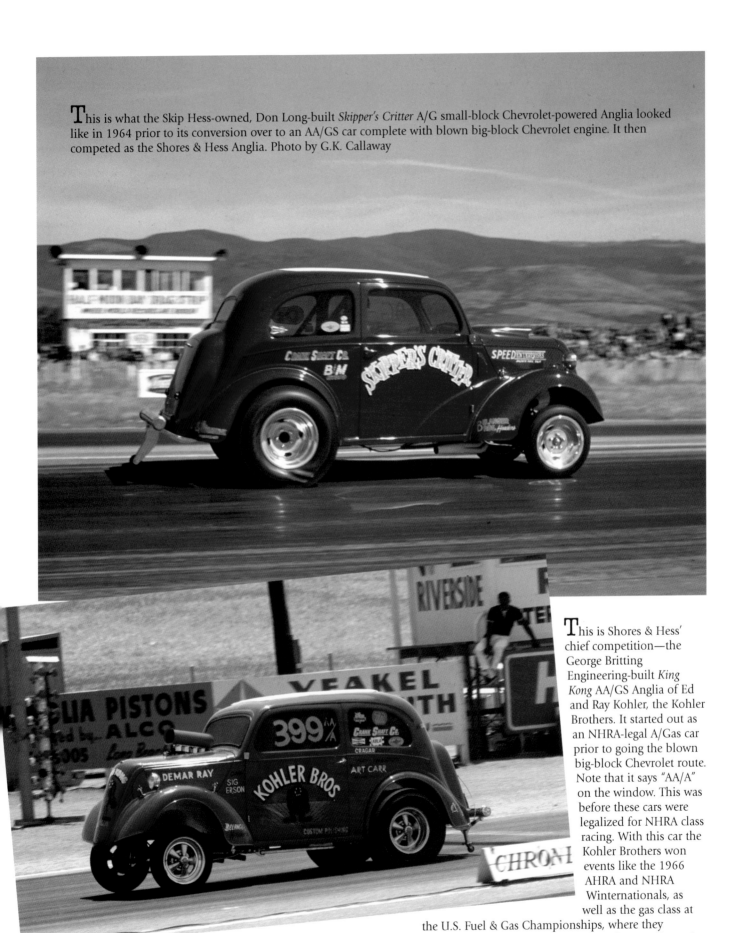

This is what the Skip Hess-owned, Don Long-built *Skipper's Critter* A/G small-block Chevrolet-powered Anglia looked like in 1964 prior to its conversion over to an AA/GS car complete with blown big-block Chevrolet engine. It then competed as the Shores & Hess Anglia. Photo by G.K. Callaway

This is Shores & Hess' chief competition—the George Britting Engineering-built *King Kong* AA/GS Anglia of Ed and Ray Kohler, the Kohler Brothers. It started out as an NHRA-legal A/Gas car prior to going the blown big-block Chevrolet route. Note that it says "AA/A" on the window. This was before these cars were legalized for NHRA class racing. With this car the Kohler Brothers won events like the 1966 AHRA and NHRA Winternationals, as well as the gas class at the U.S. Fuel & Gas Championships, where they defeated Doug "Cookie" Cook by recording a best of 9.12-seconds. Today, a collector in New York State owns this car and it is undergoing a full restoration. Photo by G.K. Callaway

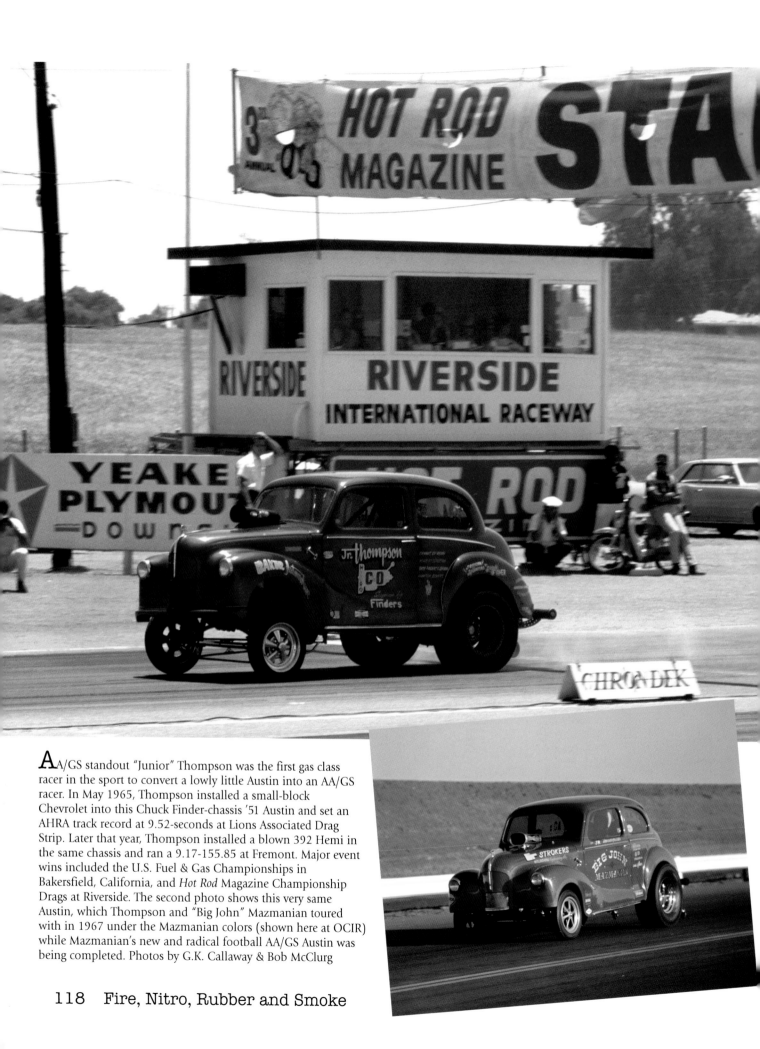

AA/GS standout "Junior" Thompson was the first gas class racer in the sport to convert a lowly little Austin into an AA/GS racer. In May 1965, Thompson installed a small-block Chevrolet into this Chuck Finder-chassis '51 Austin and set an AHRA track record at 9.52-seconds at Lions Associated Drag Strip. Later that year, Thompson installed a blown 392 Hemi in the same chassis and ran a 9.17-155.85 at Fremont. Major event wins included the U.S. Fuel & Gas Championships in Bakersfield, California, and *Hot Rod* Magazine Championship Drags at Riverside. The second photo shows this very same Austin, which Thompson and "Big John" Mazmanian toured with in 1967 under the Mazmanian colors (shown here at OCIR) while Mazmanian's new and radical football AA/GS Austin was being completed. Photos by G.K. Callaway & Bob McClurg

In 1971, Southern California racer Ed Middlebrook built this 365-ci Chrysler-powered '51 Austin BB/GS car, which also competed in CC/A. Named *Myth*, the two-tone purple Austin ran a best of 9.58-145.00 as an NHRA-legal gasser and 8.57-162.00 as an altered. This photo of Middlebrook was taken at Lions Associated Drag Strip in late 1972.

Because Anglia panel trucks carried a little more weight over the rear wheels than the sedans, the little English Fords made excellent gas class race cars. Take, for example, the Conant Brothers Competition Sales-sponsored panel seen here in action at the NHRA Springnationals at Dallas Motor Speedway, circa 1970, where the small-block Chevrolet engine C/Gas Anglia ran an 11.67 breakout.

Another example of an Anglia panel, albeit with a chopped top, is the Centerville, Ontario-based *Fast Eddy* A/GS, sponsored by Karbelt Automotive Center. The car is seen here in competition at the 1967 NHRA U.S. Nationals in Indianapolis. Photo by G.K. Callaway

Here's the "football," owned by "Big John" Mazmanian. This car appeared on the cover of *Hot Rod* Magazine and was built by Ron Scrima's Exhibition Engineering. The Dick Bourgeois- and later Rich Siroonian-driven Austin featured a lift-off body and a Dave Zeuschel-built 427-ci Chrysler engine. This car was capable of times in the 8.60s (best of 8.61-seconds) and terminal speeds of 161.87 mph. Photo by G.K. Callaway

A big-block Ford powered this A/Gas IHRA racer named the *Blue Angel*. The car ran in the high 8s and did some really nice wheelies.

The little H and I/Gas *Inch Pincher* Volkswagen of Darrell Vittone and Dean Lowry could only run in the low 13s at 102.00, but that was more than enough to win its fair share of Modified Eliminator races, including the *Hot Rod* Magazine Championship Drags at Riverside. Joe Vitton's European Motors and Engineered Motor Parts Incorporated (EMPI, as it is more commonly known with high-performance VW fans) sponsored the car.

Here's "Ohio George" Montgomery's revolutionary Malco Gasser, the '67 Mustang that forever changed the face of gasser racing—or some might say killed it! The confusion began once everybody started building late-model-bodied cars. People asked, "Are these faster gassers or just slower Funny Cars?" Photo by G.K. Callaway

In light of "Ohio George" Montgomery's successful debut of his '67 AA/GS Ford Mustang, others followed. For example, pictured is Ron Hassel's *Mr. Gasket Test Car* '67 blown big-block Chevrolet Camaro AA/GS caught in action at the NHRA Winternationals in Pomona, California. However, the car wasn't nearly as successful as Montgomery's Mustang was.

This late 1960s shot was taken of Doolin & Stroupe's Chrysler-powered AA/GS Corvette going up against Vern Hicks' *West Coast Gambler* '68 Chrysler-Mustang AA/GS at Sacramento Raceway. Ideally, times for these cars were in the mid 8s at 165+ mph.

Jeff and Larry Storck campaigned this neat little copper and orange flamed 305-ci Chevrolet-powered Opel GT BB/GS (with a Lenco four-speed transmission) at NHRA National events from 1972 through 1976. In 1973, the car set an NHRA E.T. record at 9.27-seconds. Ultimately the car ran a best of 8.96-159.00. This photo was taken of Larry Storck at the 1973 NHRA U.S. Nationals at Indianapolis Raceway Park.

Although most of the "new-breed gassers" were either Mustangs, Camaros, Barracudas, or Corvettes, every once in awhile you had something unique like this '69 Dodge Dart, campaigned by none other than "Bad Brad" Anderson. Anderson's Dart was powered by a gasoline-burning blown 426 Hemi and ran a best of 8.77 at 160 mph. Anderson went on to field two or three more blown gassers, all painted Anderson's adopted candy apple red. Photo by G.K. Callaway

In 1969, former Willys BB/GS racer "Lil' John" Lombardo stepped up to a Jim Kirby-Challenger Race Cars-built AA/GS roadster powered by a blown 420-ci Chrysler Hemi. Lombardo flat-out dominated the local West Coast AA/GS shows, running 8.50s at 169 mph. Then it was on to a whole series of Lombardo AA/Fuel Funny Cars. Photo by G.K. Callaway

In the late 1960s, Central California gas class racers Teixiera Brothers & Dad pulled the body off their late Hemi-powered A/Gas '41 Willys coupe and installed this '61 Corvette body in its place. Fred Teixiera drove the Hemi 'Vette to numerous Street Eliminator wins, running as quick as 9.75-seconds at 148.00 mph.

Late-model Mopars made huge inroads into gas class racing in the early 1970s. Shown in these two photos are the Van Gorder & Roell B/Gas '69 Hemi 'Cuda and Sam Gianino's Gratiot Auto Supply B/Gas '70 Hemi Challenger.

The popular Buick import, the Opel, also continued to be a popular body style throughout the gas classes, as witnessed by this side-by-side race photo of a pair of lower gas class machines.

This night shot of Walker & Geary versus the *Monkey Motion* was taken at Fontana Drag City in the summer of 1964. Note that a blown small-block Chevrolet powers the *Monkey Motion*. Photo by G.K. Callaway

A blown Chrysler was substituted for *Monkey Motion's* small-block Chevrolet in 1965. Driven by numerous drivers, including Ron McKibben, Bob Gregg, Maurie Hoover, Jim Miles, and Ray Higley, the *Monkey Motion* Bantam ran a career best of 7.59-199.54. Photo by G.K. Callaway

"Wild Willie" Borsch is in action at Lions Associated Drag Strip (LADS) around 1964. The Harrell, Borsch & Muse (and later Harrell & Borsch) *Winged Express* began life in 1960 as a 10-second blown gas altered. Five years later, the car was running 8.84-177.56 while competing in the Top Gas Eliminator bracket for a $150 savings bond at Lions. By 1969, the then-Marcellus & Borsch *Winged Express* had run as quick as 7.29-seconds at over 200 mph! Photo by G.K. Callaway

This shot of Rich Guasco's small-block Chevrolet engine *Pure Hell* AA/FA with Dale "Snail" Emery behind the wheel was taken at the 1964 *Hot Rod* Magazine Championship Drag Races at Riverside International Raceway, where the car won the AA/HR class. Photo by G.K. Callaway

This is Danny Collins shoeing the Campos Brothers Scotty Fenn-chassis *Lo Blow* Chevrolet AA/FA. The reason why the car was named *Lo Blow* was because the '27 T-bodied altered originally was powered by a 292-cid, fuel-burning Potvin front-mounted blown Chevrolet small-block engine. The *Lo Blow* was good for 8.9s at 170.00 mph. Photo by G.K. Callaway

This metal flake gold and red flamed '41 Willys coupe looks more like a blown gasser than an altered. However, with a direct drive early Chrysler Hemi on nitro, the Bill Hendersen-owned, Johnny Lee-driven *Fantasia* Willys was classified as an NHRA-legal AA/FA. Photo by G.K. Callaway

Frank "Hawk" Harris lights 'em up in the Bradford's 427 Chevrolet AA/FA. Originally an injected nitro car, Dexter and Randy Bradford switched over to a blown Chevrolet in 1968, running low 7s at 192.00 mph.

In the summer of 1969, *Lo Blow II* driver Tom Ferraro was critically burned when the Richard Campos-tuned fuel Chrysler Hemi engine let go in the lights, engulfing car and driver in a hellacious inferno. Ferraro got the roadster stopped but not before suffering burns over 60 percent of his body. He would spend more than a year in the hospital recuperating. Photo by G.K. Callaway

RIGHT: In 1968, Gary Reed drove car owner/driver Glenn "Groundshaker" Way's *Groundshaker Jr.* Woody Gilmore-chassis AA/FA to a new NHRA Top Speed and E.T. record of 7.68-201.34 using a Glen Okazaki-tuned blown 392 Hemi. When Reed didn't drive, Way did, as shown here at the 1969 Bakersfield March Meet. Tom Ferraro also briefly drove this car in early 1969 and recorded a top-end speed of 207.00 at OCIR. Photo by G.K. Callaway

The Northern California-based team of the Burkholder Bros., with brother "Hairy" Burkholder (yes, that's how he spelled it) behind the wheel, ran a number of unique altereds including a '23 T touring and this candy green and white Fiat Topolino, which ran a best of 7.06 at 210.00 mph. This car has recently been restored and is making the rounds at the Southern California drag racing nostalgia meets.

In 1972, professional glazier and fuel-altered handler Dennis Geisler in the Graf & Geisler *Instant T* AA/FA ran a 7.29-230.00 to become the fastest AA/FA in captivity. Geisler, of course, went on to drive Funny Cars, with the most memorable ride being in Bert Berniker's *Hindsight* rear-engine Plymouth Duster at Pomona.

The team of Mondello & Matsubara ran two Fiat fuel altereds during its illustrious career. The second car, this Exhibition Engineering Fiat Topolino, ran a best of 7.75-seconds at 192.70 mph. This car has been found recently and is undergoing a complete restoration. Photo by G.K. Callaway

Contrary to popular belief, California didn't have a stranglehold on fuel-altered racing. Here's a case in point. This shot of the Midwest's Gretchko Brothers' Austin Bantam was taken at the NHRA U.S. Nationals at Indianapolis in 1971, where the 392 early-Hemi engine altered ran a 6.99-seconds.

Here's the late-Hemi-powered Rosen & Schumacher *Altered Ego* AA/FA at Indy, circa 1968-69. This was before the team repainted its Ramchargers-engine altered car with the familiar black and white stripe motif. Prior to its retirement, this car ran a 6.98.

Mac McCord's *Go-Rilla* was a classic example of a funny style, or new breed AA/FA, with its low-slung long wheelbase chassis and aerodynamic treatments. This car ran in the mid to high 6s with late-model power and competed at the Fuel Altered Nationals at Tucson Dragway.

One of drag racing's most popular blown alcohol altereds was Sherm Gunn's Lawce Bros. & Gunn-M&S Welding T-bodied AA/A, powered by an Earl Wade-built gasoline-burning big-block Chevrolet. One of Gunn's trademarks was his habit of carrying off the front wheels to the eighth mile. This car was the first gasoline-burning altered into the 7s in NHRA competition, posting a 7.99 at Lions Associated Drag Strip on November 6, 1971. Prior to Sherm Gunn's departure to Funny Cars, the Lawce Bros. & Gunn AA/A ran a best of 7.2-seconds on alcohol.

One of the most popular lower class altereds in 1970s NHRA sportsman drag racing was Joe Williamson's Gumout-sponsored, Ford straight-six engine E/A. Joe checks out this photographer while speeding along at 143.00 mph through the lights at Pomona Raceway, circa 1972. And hello to you too, Joe!

In the late 1970s, lower-class altered racing experienced a resurgence mainly due to the implementation of modern-age technology, like late-model Hemi engines and trick Funny Car-style transmissions. Here's a shot of Don Scott's 7-second A/A going up against Gene Adams and Don Enriquez during Competition Eliminator action at the U.S. Nationals.

Wheels-up action typified the lower-class altereds, like the Will's Cargo late *Hemi-fied* A/A.

Undoubtedly the East Coast's answer to Sherm Gunn was Tony Terenzio driving the *Let It Fly* AA/A Chrysler-T, seen here in action against K.S. Pittman's AA/GS Opel at the 1971 NHRA Summernationals at Raceway Park. Starting line wheelies and speeds in the low 200s were commonplace.

NHRA Division 4 altered driver Roy Rastetter and his late-model Hemi A/A were often the class of the field with performances like a best of 9.43-143.00. This thing kind of looks like a Funny Car without the body, doesn't it?

The Mori Brothers' big-block Chevrolet-powered B/A *Chevwagon* VW altered ran both the NHRA Division 1 and IHRA circuit for many, many years. The car ran in the high 9s and low 10s.

Ah, diversity. That's one of the things that makes drag racing so great! This Dodge Colt station wagon may seem like an unlikely candidate for an altered, but it is one. The Stickle & Noltmeyer *Rod Shop* competed in the D/Altered class powered by a Gurney Westlake Eagle Dodge "Indy" motor, which propelled the little grocery-getter to low 10-second times.

Another example of an altered benefiting from late-model engine technology was the (John) Morey & (Frank) Pettinalo *Rat Poison* A/FA, which was the IHRA class record holder at 7.61-seconds at 191.68 mph.

This is former *Popular Cars* magazine editor Jim Kelso competing at the 1985 NHRA Winternationals with his blown big-block Chevrolet engine *Shutterbug* S/C VW, which ran in the high 8s. This is the same chassis that Kelso won Super Comp with the following year as a T-bodied A/Altered.

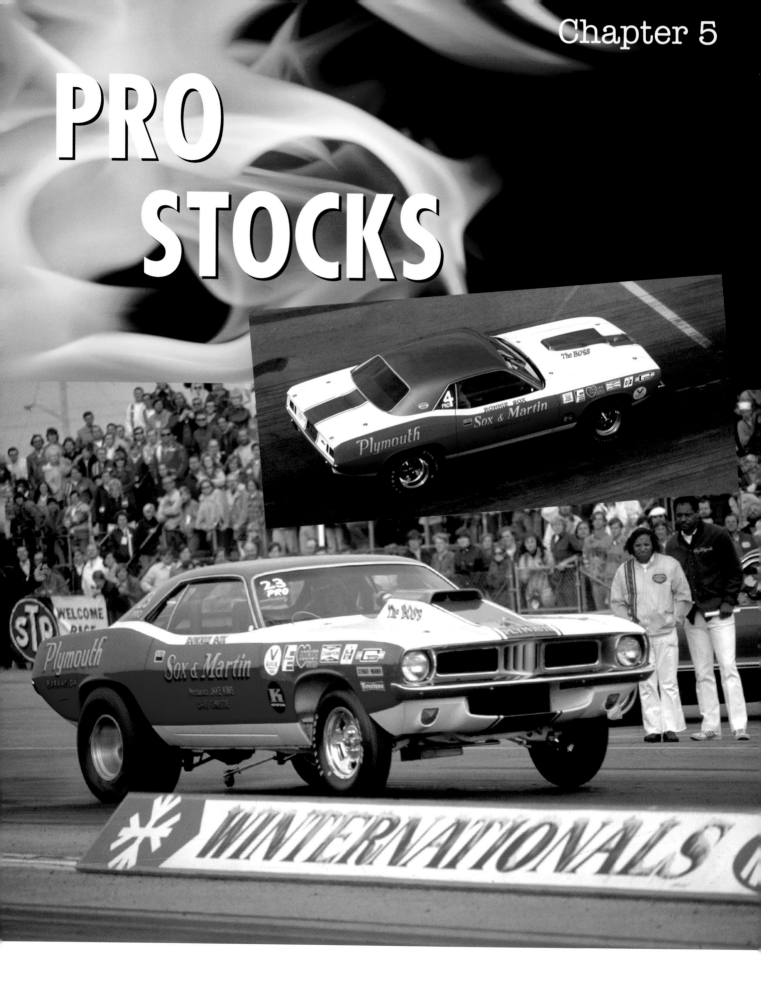

PRO STOCKS

April 22, 2006, marked the passing of one of drag racing's fiercest competitors, Ronnie Sox. Whether he was racing Super Stock, A/FX, Funny Car, or Pro Stock, Sox was universally acknowledged as one of the best four-speed men in the business, and the team of Sox & (Buddy) Martin was always on top of its game.

Although Sox & Martin is principally known for its red, white, and blue Mopars, the pair started out racing a '63 Z11 R-Code Chevrolet Impala SS. In 1964, after Chevrolet pulled out of racing, the team switched over to Mercury, fielding one of 11 lightweight 427 Mercury Comet A/FX cars, which Sox drove to the Factory Stock Eliminator title at the 1964 NHRA Winternationals. The team was also the first A/FX car in the 10s that year (10.98) and Sox & Martin closed out the 1964 season as members of the United States Drag Racing Team that toured Great Britain.

The following year marked the beginning of Sox & Martin's long association with the Chrysler Corporation, with the acquisition of one of five hand-built altered wheelbase A/FX match race Plymouths, which later became known as Funny Cars. Again Sox & Martin dominated the class. The team held the distinction of being the first carbureted match race Mopar in the 9s, and the first injected match race Mopar in the 8s.

In 1966, Sox & Martin continued its winning ways with the debut of the famous Barracuda Mopar match racer that ran low 9s on gasoline and a four-speed, and high 8s on nitro with an automatic. That's about the time I became acquainted with Sox and Martin. I had heard that all the touring Funny Car racers hung out at the Marco Polo Motel across the street from Disneyland in Anaheim, and that included Sox & Martin. One morning after the *Drag Strip* magazine East Versus West Funny Car Championships at Lions Associated Drag Strip, I drove over to the Marco Polo and found Ronnie Sox out in the parking lot. We struck up a conversation, and I more or less invited myself along to ride with the team up to Doug's Headers in East Los Angeles, where they were having their Barracuda outfitted with a new set of headers. At the time, Doug's Headers sponsored practically every top-name match race team in the business (Sox & Martin; "Dandy Dick" Landy; Hubert Platt; Stone, Woods & Cook; "Big John" Mazmanian, etc.), so this proved to be a golden opportunity for a budding young drag racing photographer like myself to meet and greet, in spite of the fact that I had no idea how I was going to get back home that evening. Fortunately for me, I was able to hitch a ride back to Anaheim with Mopar racer "Pee Wee" Wallace.

Sox & Martin abandoned the Funny Car ranks in 1967 with the institution of the Chrysler Corporation's highly successful Super Car Performance Clinic program(s), which toured the country for the next six seasons. During that time, the team of Sox & Martin set and re-set the NHRA speed and E.T. records in every class in which it competed. In the process, Sox won five straight NHRA Springnationals titles (Super Stock and Pro Stock combined), a record that remains unbroken. The team also won Super Stock Eliminator in all but one NHRA National event in 1969 with its '68 SS/A Hemi 'Cuda, not only earning the NHRA Super Stock World Championship crown but also the $5,000 cash bonus posted by George Hurst of Hurst Performance.

However, while the Sox & Martin team was extremely successful at winning national events, it excelled at "run what ya brung" southern-style match racing. In 1969, Sox & Martin got together with "Dyno Don" Nicholson, Dick Landy, and Bill "Grumpy" Jenkins to form the United States Drag Racing Team, a heads-up, match race Super Stock circuit that was so successful that the NHRA created its "new for 1970" Pro Stock Eliminator class with the USDRT's rules as guidelines.

Of course, Jenkins' '68 ZL1-engine Camaro won the inaugural Pro Stock title against Sox at the 1970 NHRA Winternationals, but the remainder of the season as well as the following year (1971) of NHRA Pro Stock was dominated by the red, white and blue Mopars of Sox & Martin.

During its heyday, Sox & Martin won a total of five NHRA, AHRA, and IHRA Pro Stock World Championships. The team was invited to the White House in 1972 to meet President Richard M. Nixon. Sox & Martin also operated a race shop in Burlington, North Carolina, which boasted numerous winning Mopar customer cars belonging to the likes of Reid Whisnant, Bobby Yowell, Ronald Lyle, and others.

Bill "Grumpy" Jenkins won the very first NHRA Pro Stock Eliminator title against Ronnie Sox at the 1970 NHRA Winternationals driving his *Grumpy's Toy V*, a '68 ZL1-engined Chevrolet Camaro, which was the same car Jenkins had run successfully on the United States Drag Racing Team circuit racing against the likes of Sox & Martin, "Dandy Dick" Landy, and "Dyno Don" Nicholson. However, Jenkins sold the Camaro shortly after his victory at Pomona to Brooklyn, New York, street racer "Brooklyn Heavy" for an undisclosed sum of cash, reportedly delivered to Jenkins in brown paper bags. In its place, Jenkins substituted *Grumpy's Toy VI*, a 427 ZL1-engine '69 COPO Camaro Super Stock car that had been converted over to Pro Stock specs. However, the 1969 car wasn't nearly as competitive as the 1968 car had been, and Jenkins spent the remainder of the season watching Sox & Martin do all the winning.

With the founding of Pro Stock Eliminator, 1964 NHRA Winternationals Super Stock champ Butch "California Flash" Leal found himself starting out the season racing Mickey Thompson's Boss 429-powered '70 Mach-1 Mustang. Then, with the release of the second generation '70 Chevrolet Camaros, Leal built one of these cars. However, the car never seemed to live up to Leal's expectations and was sold in the early part of the 1971 season after Leal accepted a lucrative offer to return to Mopar.

One of the best known independent Mopar racers from 1971 was Dayton, Ohio's Billy "The Kid" Stepp and his Paul Frost-prepared '71 Dodge Challenger. Both Don Carlton and Stuart McDade drove this car to numerous local NHRA Division 3 wins. In fact, Carlton set the NHRA Speed and Low E.T. record with this car in the fall of 1971 at 9.58-144.57. Unfortunately, Stepp's Challenger never quite made it to the big show.

Atlanta plumber Reid Whisnant was another Sox & Martin customer who fared well with his '70–'71 Plymouth Duster. Whisnant won the NHRA Division 2 Pro Stock Points Championship with this car, which routinely ran in the mid to high 9s in the 140+-mph range. Today, his son Mark Whisnant carries on the family tradition racing in NHRA Pro Stock.

In the early days of Pro Stock, the Ford flag was carried into battle by "Dyno Don" Nicholson and his 427 SOHC Ford Mavericks, which ran in the high 9s at 140 mph. In this photo taken at the 1971 NHRA Summernationals, he twists the front end of his M&S Race Cars-built '71 Maverick coming off the starting line. Nicholson was nothing but tough.

Although York, Pennsylvania's Bill Stiles (Stiles Performance) gained his reputation as one of the East Coast's finest Mopar Super Stock racers, he too jumped onto the Pro Stock bandwagon with this '70 Plymouth Duster, seen here racing Bill Blanding's *Mimi* Camaro at Capitol Raceway in the summer of 1971. Stiles' wheels-up performances always endeared him to early Pro Stock fans.

In mid 1971, Butch "California Flash" Leal stopped flogging his big-block Chevrolet Camaro and built this Ron Butler-chassis Plymouth Duster, which proved the scourge of NHRA Division 7 Pro Stock ranks. Of course, part of Leal's agreement with Chrysler was that he would also attend the NHRA National events. Here we see Leal getting some serious air at the 1971 NHRA-Le Grandnational-Molson in Sanair, Canada.

Although Ford had most of its hopes riding on "Dyno Don" Nicholson in the early days of Pro Stock Eliminator, Dick Brannan was nonetheless still recognized as the captain of the Ford Drag Team. Brannan is shown here qualifying his 427 SOHC Maverick at Indy 1970, an event won by Sox & Martin.

MIDDLE: Bill "Grumpy" Jenkins celebrated his second year of Pro Stock Eliminator racing with the release of his new *Grumpy's Toy VIII*, a big-block '71 Camaro seen here in competition at the NHRA Winternationals. In truth, this car proved a better match racer than it did an NHRA-legal Pro Stock car, running 9.50s with ease. Of course, this is the same car that was rented to Bruce "USA-1" Larson in 1972 and then sold to Richie Zul who, with a ton of updating by SRD Race Cars, won the 1974 NHRA Summernationals. This car was restored by noted Midwestern muscle car collector Mike Gaurise and is shown on the Chevrolet nostalgia circuit.

BELOW: This shot of "Brooklyn Heavy's" Carmen Rotunda-driven 1970 Chevrolet Pro Stock Camaro was taken at the 1971 *Cars* Magazine Championships in Atco, New Jersey. Although this Diamond Racing Engines-equipped Camaro was an NHRA-legal Pro Stock car, it more than likely spent more time racing on the street.

This is one of my all-time favorite Pro Stock pictures taken of Roy "Hill Billy" Hill driving his Petty Enterprises-built '73 Plymouth Duster Pro Stocker during an eight-car match race at Capitol Raceway in Maryland. Aside from the incredible starting launch, the look of determination on Hill's face is priceless! His new Duster was one of two drag race cars ever built by Petty Enterprises. The other car was the King's '65 Plymouth Barracuda (a.k.a. *43 Jr.*), which Petty campaigned briefly during the infamous Chrysler-NASCAR boycott of 1965. Of course, Hill is best known these days for his drag racing school. Today, a collector living in Southern California owns Hill's one-off Petty Engineering-built Duster, and it's being restored.

Although the Mopars of Butch Leal and Bill Bagshaw more or less controlled NHRA Division 7 West Coast Pro Stock racing, there were other Mopar teams who competed on this level but never were recognized for their contributions. One such example was San Dimas, California's Jim Clark driving the Engine Dynamics *Hemi Express* Dodge Demon, seen here in competition at OCIR in 1973. This car ran in the mid to high 9s at 145 mph, and as you can see, it was a first-class effort.

In 1971, Dick Maskin and Dave Kanners went Pro Stock racing with this 401 engine AMC Gremlin, which, in spite of its short wheelbase and zero aerodynamics, ran high 9s. The next year they campaigned the phenomenally successful *Hornet-X*, which ran in the high 8s.

Bill "Grumpy" Jenkins may have fielded the first successful Vega Pro Stock car, but others followed. One such example is that of former AHRA GT champs Hiner & Miller and its Keystone Wheels-sponsored, Dick Lowry-constructed 327 engine Pro Stock '72 Chevrolet Vega, which turned a 9.70 at 140 mph with Jerry Miller doing the driving.

This is "Whiteland Bob" Glidden's (Glidden & Allen) second Pro Stock Ford Pinto, built by Norm Paddack Race Cars. This is the car Glidden used to run an 8.69-152.28 and win his first NHRA Pro Stock World Championship at Ontario 1974, as well as to finish in the runner-up spot to Wayne Gapp, running an 8.96-152.80 to Gapp's 8.87-152.08.

In an attempt to change his fortunes competing in NHRA Pro Stock, long-time Mopar clinic racer Don Grotheer had Don Hardy build this new Pro Stock Pinto in 1973 that ran 9.20s. By then, though, Grotheer had tired of the whole rat race. Shortly thereafter, he sold the car and went cattle ranching.

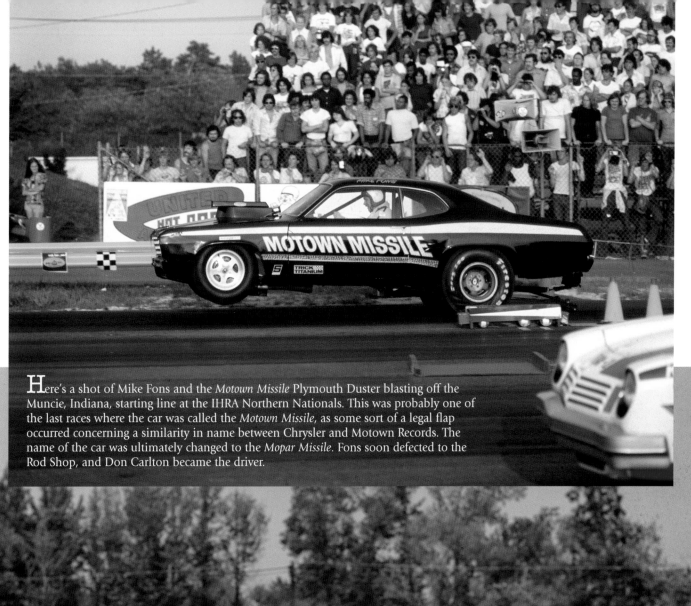

Here's a shot of Mike Fons and the *Motown Missile* Plymouth Duster blasting off the Muncie, Indiana, starting line at the IHRA Northern Nationals. This was probably one of the last races where the car was called the *Motown Missile*, as some sort of a legal flap occurred concerning a similarity in name between Chrysler and Motown Records. The name of the car was ultimately changed to the *Mopar Missile*. Fons soon defected to the Rod Shop, and Don Carlton became the driver.

In 1972, Jeg Coughlin built a new Vega, which he raced both nationally and in NHRA Division 3. However, event wins eluded old Coughlin, and the following year he built a Ford Pinto to race instead.

Butch Leal lays down a smoke screen at Indy 1973 driving his brand new Ron Butler Race Cars-built Plymouth Duster. This car ran a 9.14-150.50 at Indy 1973 to nail down Low E.T. for Mopars.

This head-on shot of Bobby Yowell driving Billy "Kid" Stepp's #2 Dodge Demon was taken at the 1973 NHRA U.S. Nationals using a Hasselblad 120 camera outfitted with a 500-mm telephoto lens. I just loved those days when the NHRA used to let photographers do what we did best!

Chevy Funny Car driver "Professor Kelly" Chadwick went Pro Stock racing in 1974 with this Don Hardy-built Chevrolet Vega, which ran a best of 9.30-146.80 the first time out.

Bob Riffle drives the Rod Shop Dodge Demon hard off the Rockingham, North Carolina, starting line. Riffle assumed control of this ride after Mike Fons vacated the driver's seat.

When Don Carlton wasn't driving the *Mopar Missile,* he often drove his own car, which competed in both IHRA Pro Stock and the IHRA altered classes.

This is "Dyno Don" Nicholson with one of his most inspired race cars, his long wheelbase '70 Mach-1 Mustang Pro Stocker, which was runner-up at the 1974 NHRA U.S. Nationals. There the car ran 9.01, 8.96, 8.99, 8.96, and 9.01 E.T. speeds to finish in behind "Whiteland Bob" Glidden. Nicholson was a real innovator and a helluva racer. We all sure miss him.

NHRA-Winston Pro Stock World Champion "Whiteland Bob" Glidden was another of the Ford racers to take advantage of the NHRA rules in 1974 and had Don Hardy build him the sister car to "Dyno Don" Nicholson's Mustang. Glidden won quite a few races with this car, including Columbus and Englishtown. However, by the NHRA Finals there was a new Don Hardy Pinto that Glidden used to complete in the championship quest.

These days you hear a lot of talk about female NHRA Pro Stock racer Erica Enders. However, the young lady driving this Pro Stock Dodge Demon was NHRA Division 4's very first female Pro Stock pilot, Abilene, Texas' Shay Nichols, one-half of the Shay and Phil Nichols racing team. She's driving her Shelby Jester-tuned, Joe Smith Race Cars-constructed Dodge Demon.

Ronnie Sox drives "Rapid Ronald" Lyles' Dodge Colt at the 1974 PRA Race held at New York National Speedway in Center Moriches, Long Island, New York. These Colts were a handful to drive, but if anybody could get 'er down the track, it was Sox!

Here's New York racer Richie Zul driving the ex-Bill "Grumpy" Jenkins big-block Camaro at the 1974 U.S. Nationals at Indianapolis Raceway Park. Zul was a strong competitor but only won one NHRA "Wally" throughout his career. However, he picked the right race to win, as Zul won Pro Stock Eliminator at the 1974 NHRA Summernationals in front of all his "homies!"

EXHIBITION CARS

Although not considered a rear-engine dragster in the traditional sense, the "Beach Boy Jim" Busby & "Fling" Traylor rocket-powered *U.S. Turbine-1* dragster thrilled crowds in the mid 1960s with Top Fuel dragster-like performances. Two different drivers drove the *U.S. Turbine-1* dragster: George "Stone Age" Hutchinson (shown in the B&W action photo) and later "Hand Grenade Harry" Hibler, one of drag racing's early pioneers. The multi-faceted Hibler was once the manager at Old San Fernando Drag Strip, the runner-up in Top Fuel Eliminator against Tony "Loner" Nancy at the 1970 Bakersfield March Meet, and one time publisher of *Hot Rod* Magazine.

The *U.S. Turbine-1* was powered by a "Turbinique" turbine engine hooked up to a conventional rear axle. The car left the starting line with a huge "pow" while producing a flame trail and smoking the tires like a conventional Top Fuel dragster. Unfortunately, the car never lived up to expectations, and according to Hibler (who ran 218.00 with the car), it was like driving either a midget or sprint car with two different sized rear tires!

Rumor had it that in later years, the *U.S. Turbine-1's* Speed Products Engineering (SPE) chassis was back halved into a conventional rear engine dragster. Color photos by G.K. Callaway. Action photo courtesy Alan Earman

Linda Vaughn is nationally renown as the "First Lady of Motorsports." The Dalton, Georgia-born woman first burst onto the scene in the early 1960s as an 18-year-old trophy girl at NASCAR races, serving as "Miss Atlanta Motor Speedway." Linda's natural southern sweetness blended with her incredible physical architecture, and her patented "Hey y'all" greeting landed her gigs with Pontiac and as a trophy girl at the original Nassau Speed Weeks events. In the early 1960s, Vaughn was "Miss Firebird" for the Pure Oil Company, which at the time was the official fuel provider for NASCAR.

You might say that Vaughn's career kicked into high gear when she met George Hurst through an introduction arranged by her mother, Mae, and NHRA Chief Starter and former NHRA Division 2 director Eddie "Buster" Couch. Hurst was particularly impressed with how the articulate Vaughn mingled with the fans and sponsors alike, making them all feel like they were one big, happy family. Vaughn's debut as "Miss Hurst Golden Shifter" at the 1964 NHRA Winternationals marked the beginning of a 35-plus-year association with Hurst Performance. Vaughn made personal appearances at drag racing events throughout the country, riding on the platform of an Oldsmobile convertible outfitted with a 15-foot-high Hurst shifter! Vaughn also made personal appearances at Indy and at select NASCAR events. Throughout it all, she traveled more than 100,000 miles a year.

"I've made more passes (down the quarter mile) than a desperate old maid school teacher," Vaughn once commented in *Car Craft* magazine in 1967 with a huge smile.

As a testosterone-laden youth, I read about Vaughn in the magazines and admired her from afar. However, I was finally able to meet her in person at the 1968 NHRA U.S. Nationals at Indianapolis while working for Fram Corporation as their event photographer. That was the first of many meetings that we had. As my career progressed, she often took me aside at the drag races and gave me a few pointers. "Hey, little brother, you know, you 'oughta do this, and this . . ."

Vaughn attempted to get me hired at Hurst Performance on a number of occasions and was able to arrange an interview for me with George Hurst and Jack Duffy, who seemed to be more than impressed with my credentials. Unfortunately, there was a gentleman in the chain of command at the Warminster, Pennsylvania-based shifter empire who felt that I might be a threat to his job, so nothing ever came of it.

Probably one of the most memorable stories of Vaughn that I have is from 1971, when I was working as the public relations man for Dayton, Ohio, Pro Stock racer Bobby Yowell. In those days, the Yowell family had a United Van Lines franchise. One day, Vaughn called me up to tell me that she was moving to California. She suggested that perhaps it might be good publicity for Yowell Movers, Inc. to relocate the "First Lady of Drag Racing" from Atlanta to her new home in Newport Beach, California. Company president Neil T. Yowell jumped at the idea, and before I knew it I was on my way down to Vaughn's apartment in Atlanta to supervise the move.

Suffice to say, Vaughn's promotional-minded business savvy, incredible looks, and down-home manners kept her at the forefront of one of the fastest changing sports in the country a heck of a lot longer than most people. For example, after noting that the fans had grown complacent with seeing her make her customary pass down the quarter mile on the back of the Hurst Shifter car, Vaughn freshened up the act by introducing the "Hurst-ettes," which included the likes of former *Playboy* Playmates of the Month June Cochran, Shelly Harmon, Tammy Pittman (daughter of gasser great K.S. Pittman), and Eloise Coulter.

In the late 1990s, after Vaughn had retired as "Miss Hurst Golden Shifter," she signed on with the NHRA at national events, where she did a fabulous job as a "color commentator." Although she and I no longer travel in the same circles, we still see each other occasionally and keep in contact by telephone, where she keeps trying to marry me up to her younger sister Shelia! You might say it's just an ongoing "thang" we have!

In the early 1980s, "Jet Jockey" Bob Motz campaigned this jet engine Kenworth tractor around the country. Powered by a Westinghouse J47 jet engine, this behemoth used to run a top speed of 207 mph, which in a weird sort of way was almost anticlimactic compared to the fire show Motz put on at the starting line "with burner pops" and flames shooting out of the stacks. I shot this photo at Houston Dragway one summer evening in 1980, which was no easy task. Motz put out so much heat and flame that it singed my beard!

Here's a shot of Les Shockley's *Shock Wave* jet dragster at OCIR sometime around 1978. Shockley started out as Hayden Proffitt's chief mechanic in the old Funny Car days, prior to becoming involved with jets. The *Shock Wave* ran in the mid 250s with ease. But what's probably even more surprising is the fact that Proffitt bought the jet car from Les and campaigned it himself at the ripe old age of 65!

This is Ray "Engine Masters" Alley driving the Jim Lytle-built *Big Al* Allison-engine '34 Ford Tudor Sedan at Fontana Drag City sometime around 1963 or 1964.

"I paid one dollar per cubic inch for that car, $1,100," said Alley. Ray campaigned the '34 Tudor up till the time he built his first Funny Car. Then he sold it back to Jim Lytle. *Big Al* can now be seen on the drag racing nostalgia circuit. Photo by G.K. Callaway

In 1974, "Captain Jack" McClure set the drag racing world on its ear with his incredible hydrogen peroxide rocket-powered 200-mph go-kart. Sponsored by Amalie Motor Oil Co., McClure primarily ran the AHRA and IHRA circuits, where he recorded a best of 6.22-seconds at 200 mph. McClure once told me a story about the time he ran the kart at a small track in the Midwest where the guardrails were placed far back from the strip, and a strip of grass was all that separated the two. On one of his runs, a gust of wind blew the kart off the track at the eighth mile, sending McClure speeding at nearly 200 mph into the grass. "Those front spoilers acted like lawn mower blades, and there was grass flying everywhere," commented McClure. Naturally, being a journalist, I came up with the title, "The World's Fastest Lawn Mower," which McClure used for the remainder of his career when describing the sensation of speed to local newspaper reporters.

In the early 1970s, Bill Fredrick built the hydrogen peroxide rocket-powered, Wynn's Oil Company-sponsored *Courage of Australia* Land Speed Record car, which was originally driven by Vic Wilson on a 311.41-mph run on November 11, 1971, at OCIR. After Wilson quit driving, John "Peanut Butter" Paxson drove the *Courage of Australia* during the early months of testing prior to the start of the 1972 drag racing season when the team had contracted to race the IHRA circuit.

We all gathered at Irwindale Raceway (which is the current location of the Miller Brewing Company) in mid April to watch Paxson and Fredrick test, when disaster struck. A 275-mph "warm-up run" turned into the ride of Paxson's life when the parachutes failed to deploy.

"Bill had just installed a new pair of pilot chutes on the car, but they were located too close to the nozzle. The moment I deployed them, they just melted around the nozzle," Paxson said.

With no way of stopping, the *Courage of Australia* sliced through the sand traps like a hot knife through butter and continued at speed out into the rocky terrain at the end of the racetrack. Finally, the nose cone hooked on some rocks and the car flipped over the retaining fence and onto a jogger's path in the Azusa Wilderness terrain on the other side!

According to Paxson, "Wild Bill" Shrewsbury was the first one to reach him and help the uninjured Paxson climb out of the car. In the meantime, leaking hydrogen peroxide had set some of the surrounding scrub brush on fire. Then the park ranger came along, and there was a big scene!

Unfortunately, that was the end of the *Courage of Australia*. During less stressful times, the lovely Stephanie Rose posed for Wynn's Oil Company publicity pictures with the then brand-new rocket car at OCIR. Photos by G.K. Callaway & Bob McClurg

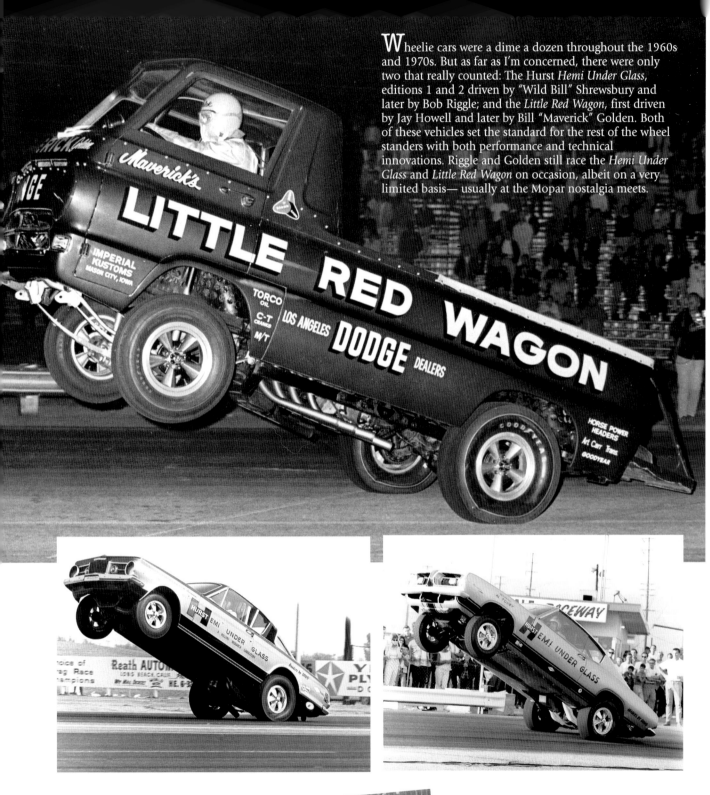

Wheelie cars were a dime a dozen throughout the 1960s and 1970s. But as far as I'm concerned, there were only two that really counted: The Hurst *Hemi Under Glass*, editions 1 and 2 driven by "Wild Bill" Shrewsbury and later by Bob Riggle; and the *Little Red Wagon*, first driven by Jay Howell and later by Bill "Maverick" Golden. Both of these vehicles set the standard for the rest of the wheel standers with both performance and technical innovations. Riggle and Golden still race the *Hemi Under Glass* and *Little Red Wagon* on occasion, albeit on a very limited basis— usually at the Mopar nostalgia meets.

Apparently, somebody forgot to bolt the axle bearing retainer plate back onto the axle housing of this '65 Mustang after making a gear change during the 1976 U.S. Nationals at Indy. Fortunately, the driver's ego was the only thing that suffered from this incident.

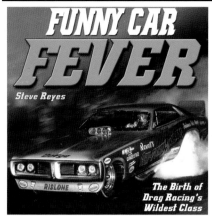
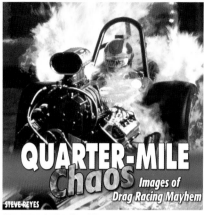
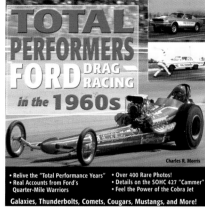
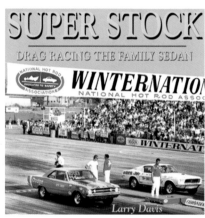
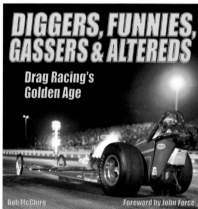